I FINALLY HAVE the SMOKING HOT BODY I HAVE ALWAYS WANTED

(having been cremated)

The woman, Alzheimer's, and the hilarious obituary that turned my dead mother into an instant worldwide celebrity.

Barb Drummond

I Finally Have the Smoking Hot Body I Have Always Wanted…
Having Been Cremated.

© Copyright 2024 By Barb Drummond

ISBN: 978-1-0689084-0-8

First Edition

Published by Barb Drummond

Publisher: Barb Drummond Writes

Website: barbdrummondwrites.com

Author photo credit: Amanda Monette

Cover photo edit: Josh Longiaru

Editor: Kim Duke

Book Cover: Rosario M. Soley

Interior Design: Virginia M. Geraige

A NOTE FROM THE AUTHOR:

This book is based on experiences compressed over a week. My mom's letters are a creative device to move the story forward. Just as I wrote Mom's obituary—I've also written her letters based on the real-life experiences (and letters) I had with her. The stories are true and although Mom had elegant handwriting, her letters have been typed to take the reader back in time and for ease of reading.

Enjoy!

MEDIA MENTIONS FOR SYBIL MARIE HICKS' OBITUARY.

Hamilton Spectator

"Sybil Hicks' obit has become a sensation, picked up all over the world and a hit on social media. It reads as though she wrote it but her kids penned it. She had Alzheimer's for 18 years."

Jim Poling @PolingRecord

The last word. Obit in today's @TheSpec

"I finally have the smoking hot body I have always wanted...having been cremated."

CBC As It Happens
"Why 'smoking hot' Sybil Hicks' children honored her with a checky first-person obituary"

Daily Mail – London England
"Her obit, though, was anything but the sad, staid affair most people expect of a death announcement."

NEWS.com.au
"A grandmother has left the world laughing after publishing a hilarious obit in which she jokes about finally having a 'smoking hot body' -post cremation."

Huffington Post
Woman's Obituary Jokes About Finally Having "Smoking Hot Body' Thanks to Cremation
"Sybil Hicks' children penned the tongue-in-cheek tribute for their mother, who was always ready for a laugh."

HEAD TOPICS United Kingdom

"Nan jokes she's 'getting a hot body' being cremated in viral obituary."

New York Post

"Woman pens her own hilarious obituary. "Sybil Hicks wrote the most hilarious first-person obituary in which she insulted her husband, her children, and had the last laugh-or so it seemed."

The Star

"Children of 'smoking' hot Sybil pen her hilarious first-person obituary."

Metro, UK

"Obituaries aren't usually fun reads. But one Canadian grandmother decided to prove that even in death, she's hilarious."

My Modern Met-New York

"Deceased Mom Becomes Posthumous Celebrity After Her Kids Publish Her Witty First Person Obituary."

The Irish Post

"OBITUARIES ARE supposed to be sombre affairs full of heartfelt tributes and expressions of sadness at the loss just experienced. But Sybil Hicks from Hamilton in Canada decided to do things a little differently when it came to the formal announcement of her own passing."

Yahoo Life

"There's one line in particular that has the internet in stitches.

"I finally have the smoking-hot body I have always wanted … having been cremated," the obituary reads."

Upworthy

"A recently deceased mom became a celebrity after her kids' published stunningly clever obituary."

"The disorder may have stolen Hicks' quick wit sharp tongue; but, in a way, the obituary has given voice to a woman who was long silenced."

Mashable

"This obituary is truly something else."

FOX8

"It's not often you read an obituary and wind up laughing, but that's exactly what the children of Sybil Marie Hicks hoped to achieve when they published hers in the Hamilton Spectator this month."

Global News

"Baysville, Ont., woman's humorous obituary, has readers laughing and crying. "One of the comments today was, 'She definitely made an ash of herself'"

This book is dedicated to my *real* Mom.

To the woman who always made the best chocolate cake, even if she couldn't always remember to grease the pans! Here's to my incredible mom, who taught me laughter is the best seasoning, even when the recipe card gets a little stained with eggs and batter.

In the grand *Fanny Farmer Cookbook* of life, you may not have always remembered the ingredients, but you sure knew how to whip up a batch of unforgettable moments.

Cheers to you, Mom, for turning most days into an unexpected adventure, and for reminding us that even when life forgets the script, it can still be one heck of a sitcom.

Thanks for the laughter, the love, and the occasional search party for the car keys and old cigarette butts.

This book is for you—because even if the details fade, the love you've given us has not.

You've proven that even in the fog of Alzheimer's, there's always room for a good laugh.

CONTENTS

CHAPTER 1:
THE CALL THAT FINALLY CAME

"Dancing with myself, ELF, oh, dancing with myself, ELF"

"What the hell is that?" I come out of a deep sleep. It was my cell phone. I fumble toward the glow — who on earth would call so early? I sit up in bed and see it's 6:13 a.m. and the caller is — my sister from three provinces away.

Now I AM curious. We haven't spoken in years. We had a falling out; I think it's ten years since we last exchanged words.

I slide my finger across the screen. "Hey," I say, my voice low and thick with sleep. It can't be good. She wouldn't call otherwise. My brothers keep me up to date on Mom and her Alzheimer's progression. A week or so ago my brother Brian told me Mom had pneumonia. Could it be?

"Hey," she says. Her voice is quiet and trembled, "I'm with Mom. The nurse said it won't be long now. She couldn't shake the pneumonia. Now is the time if you want to say goodbye."

"Ohh, fuucck," I whisper. My mind races to figure out the last time I got news on Mom. Wait, wasn't it just a week or so, was it longer since I spoke to Brian? Panic sets in. Did I visit enough? Why didn't I go back when I heard she was sick?

She didn't know me anymore.

Mom couldn't read anymore. She hadn't spoken for years. She hadn't fed or dressed herself for years. When was that exactly?

I was someone she didn't know anymore. She was someone I didn't know anymore. Guilt rears its ugly head. I feel sick to my stomach.

My voice is low and groggy. "Yes, of course, put her on."

Brenda held the phone close to Mom's ear.

"Mom, it's Barb. You remember, "Miss Perfect," I joke about my childhood nickname. *Ugh, that was stupid. Of course, she doesn't remember.*

"Mom…I just want to say thank you for being my Mom. It's okay to go. We'll be fine. You did a wonderful job with all of us kids. Dad will be fine. You'd be so proud of your grandkids. I hope there's a giant box of Carlo Rossi waiting for you. Say hi to Gramma. I love you. Bye… for now…"

I'm quiet. My body feels numb. Mom has lived with Alzheimer's for almost twenty years. It's finally taking her physical form now after taking her mentally so many years ago. I feel an odd mixture of sadness and relief— sadness for losing her and relief that her long painful battle with the memory monster has come to an end.

My sister comes back on. "Mom's gone," she whispers.

"Thanks for doing that, Brenda. Means a lot." My voice cracks and overwhelming emotions make it difficult to find the right words, any words. "I'll make arrangements and be there tomorrow if I can. There's one thing before you go, can you take a print of Mom's thumb before they take her away?"

"Uh, sure," Brenda replies.

"You know, with an ink pad. Press her thumb into it and press it onto a white piece of paper for me. I'd like to get a necklace made or something."

"So, anything else?" she asks slowly as though she really doesn't want to have to do anything else bizarre for me.

"No, that's all. Thanks. I'll keep you posted on my flight."

"K bye," she says in a hushed voice.

I hang up. No more awkward pleasantries.

It's 6:30 a.m. and I'm wide awake now. I get up to make coffee and try to process the news.

"My mom died," I say out loud. Even hearing it is hard to comprehend.

My husband, Gord, wakes up at these words. He sits up to hug me while I weep. It's strange experiencing grief for someone who "died" years before.

Mom was diagnosed at age sixty-five with early-onset dementia. I live in Western Canada and Mom and Dad live in the East. I haven't heard Mom's voice in years because of Alzheimer's.

During my trips back home each time her decline was worse.

Fresh coffee in hand I go to the living room and sit by the window. Everything feels cold. Memories of happier times with Mom flash through my mind, contrasting sharply with my last image of her in The Pines Nursing Home. She was a shell of her former vibrant self, no longer recognizing anyone around her.

When was the last time I saw Mom? I grapple with the timeline and wonder about my own memory. The last time I remember her being somewhat present was in 2006 when we first placed her in Leisure World. Mom thought she was hired as nursing staff. Which made complete sense to me as she'd been an ER nurse for years.

Dad, Brian, Brenda, and I had sat in the common room, putting on brave faces because when we left, Mom would remain.

This would now be her home.

We tried to chat over coffee and a sweet treat. Mom was having nothing to do with it. She was agitated and angry. "I don't know why I am just sitting here. I should be in the emergency room caring for patients. This coffee break is too long. This would not be acceptable at Hamilton General. I want to go home. I don't know why I put myself here!" Mom said turning her nose up in the air and looking out toward the window.

***

Fast forward to my last visit with Mom. She sat in her faded comfy chair. Her once tall, full-figured frame looked small and fragile. Her brilliance and quirky personality from her younger days were reduced to a mere shadow of her former self.

It was hard to witness.

Her deep wrinkles were etched with lines of experience and how she once loved the sun. Each crease told a story of a life well-lived, both joy and sorrow. Parts of her young face still had room for new wrinkles. Her blue eyes, once bright and full of curiosity, now held a soft faraway look that spoke of times long gone.

Her now silver hair, thin and wispy, fell gently around her face and lent her an air of grace despite the cruel invasion of Alzheimer's. I looked away and caught a glimpse of framed photos on her dresser. Smiles and laughter frozen in faded hues, our family Christmas from years ago, grandchildren blowing out birthday candles, one from their 40th-anniversary party —all reminders of a life rich with connections and experiences.

Mom sat surrounded by clues and fragments of her past, her body still a willing participant, but her mind vacant of these special memories.

***

I thought of Mom or Sybs, as we'd sometimes call her. We were such cheeky kids! I smile and remember the look on her face when we first started to refer to her by a nickname my brother coined at the grocery store when she didn't respond to "Mom!"

He called out "Sybs!", and she immediately turned and responded. It stuck!

Ah, Sybil. You were a legend. You were an exceptional woman whose brilliance radiated through your whole being.

***

In every sense, Mom was a masterpiece: a mosaic of talents, qualities, and quirks, a wonderful mother, compassionate nurse, intellectual luminary, creative soul, and a beacon of kindness. And a smart-ass sense of humour! It all formed this woman we came to know and love as Mom, Sybil, Sybs, or Mrs. Ron Hicks of Baysville.

My coffee is cold. I sigh.

At one time Mom and I were close. But as the years passed and physical distance lengthened, we were tugged further apart. Even though I spent years from home, she always found the time to write me letters when I was at university, in the Bahamas, off to Japan, or my year in Holland. It didn't matter where I went —her letters would follow.

Her letters! Of course!

In my closet is an old hatbox where I keep Mom's letters, cards, recipes, and old photos.

I decide for my long flight to Ontario, I'll bring the letters with me.

I need to hear her voice.

Old hat box.

CHAPTER 2:
THE FLIGHT, WET SOCKS, AND TWO MOTHERLESS PASSENGERS

I hastily book a flight for the next evening.

What was supposed to be a straightforward journey turns into a rollercoaster of delays, missed flights, and unexpected emotions.

My husband drives me to the airport, two hours from our home. We say our goodbyes and my journey into an unknown experience begins. I don't know what to expect. How can I? I've never lost a parent before.

The small airport buzzes with travelers. I go up to the service counter. Exhausted from a restless night, drenched from the rain, and dragging an overloaded suitcase, I offer my passport to the agent.

She stares at her screen and says, "Your flight will be delayed to Edmonton due to inclement weather."

She looks me up and down with a raised eyebrow as though I should know about the delay already since I look like a wet rag.

"Ugh, you must be kidding me. How long? I have a flight to Toronto I can't miss! THEN I have a 3-hour drive. I have a lot of moving parts here!"

As soon as the words leave my lips I think, *Oh-gawd, I am turning into one of THOSE people.*

Immediately, I try to smooth over my rude comment with, "Uhm sorry," I mutter feebly. "My mom just died, and I have a few connections and timing is critical. My brother is supposed to be on the next flight with me."

"I. can't. control. the. weather." She slowly emphasizes each word while rolling her eyes, indicating I was either a) stupid or b) this was the millionth time she'd dealt with an unhappy customer who was put out by the delay.

The way she looks at me, I think I'd have to go with a).

I text my brother that my flight is delayed and I'm not sure I can make the connection. He replies, "Don't worry. I'll wait or try and get us on the next flight out."

The staticky voice on the loudspeaker announces my flight is canceled, and the next available flight is in the late evening, hours away. Brian now has no choice but to wait.

I sit back, sigh, and wipe my tears of frustration away.

A man sitting near me asks if I'm okay. I turn to look at him – not sure how to respond. *No one REALLY wants to know when they ask, do they?*

I say quietly, "My mom just died, my flight is delayed, I hate flying and my socks are soaked. I hate wet socks."

He says, "Me too."

With a hint of surliness, I question, "You hate wet socks?"

"No," he says with a slight pause, "My mom just died."

I look at him for a few seconds, I feel my eyebrows knit together. I wonder if he's messing with me. *But no one would joke about that. Would they?*

He's sincere in his response. "Her name was Catherine. Catherine with a C. She had heart issues."

"Sorry for your loss." I offer.

"Me too," he says once again. After a bit of awkward small talk, we turn to our phones as a distraction.

When I return from the eighth visit to the ladies' room, someone has taken my spot. I wander to the far side of the waiting area. Eventually, my flight number is announced, and we board. After twelve hours in the airport, I'm not looking like my finest self.

I find my window seat.

"Well, if it isn't the lady who hates wet socks."

I glance over and laugh. Seriously, what are the odds? The gentleman who also lost his mother is assigned to the seat RIGHT beside me!

He settles in next to me, clicks his seat belt, and we quickly start talking about our mothers and what we're dealing with.

Such strange but needed healing comes from speaking to a stranger.

In Edmonton, we part at the top of the gate with a sincere goodbye and a quick comforting hug. We've shared a brief yet profound connection in our time of vulnerability and I didn't even get his name.

I find my brother talking to the gate agent when I arrive. He spots me, we hug, share tears, and sit in silence for a long time. Neither of us dare to talk for fear of more emotions spilling out, or perhaps we just don't know what to say.

Our flight is called shortly after I arrive. We board and settle in for the four-hour flight to Toronto. We look at each other and put our headphones on.

I reach into my bag and pull out one of Mom's letters.

I know she'd love my wet sock story.

October 28, 1988

Dear Barb,

I know it has been a few months since our visit, but I wanted to thank you again for the wonderful memories from our Fredericton trip this summer. Brenda and I are still smiling and of course, giggling about the "naked strangers" at the Prospect Inn!

What an unforgettable adventure on so many levels. I'll never forget the look of surprise mixed with shock when I tapped you on the shoulder at the airport and asked you for directions to find a car rental company! (Although in hindsight your horrified look was because I'd just learned you and Gord were living together.)

Driving to Halifax in the terrifying thunderstorm, eating fish and chips on the wharf; and as long as I live, I won't forget seeing the wild scary-looking guy driving toward us in Gagetown. His hair was a tangled mess, his face in such a scowl. Even behind the wheel, I could see he was a heavy-set man, and I wouldn't have wanted to meet him in a back alley. I still shiver thinking about it. When Gord piped up and said, "Hey, that's my cousin!" I admit, I thought, just who is my daughter dating?

Didn't we have a good laugh?

And I'll tell the story of walking in on the naked couple for years!! We must have scared the liver out of them! It was both mortifying and hilarious! I'm sitting here laughing about it all over again.

We had a lot of fun and I enjoyed getting to know Gord—he doesn't seem like his cousin.

I planned our surprise visit with your sister, and it came off without a hitch. You know us— "the surprise family"!

Until the next surprise, my dear.

Love,

Mom

CHAPTER 3:
SEX, LINES, AND NO VIDEOTAPE

I snort when I finish reading the letter. It wakes up my snoring brother beside me.

We're finally on our way to Toronto.

This letter is one of my favourites. The surprise visit by Mom is permanently etched in my memory.

You just can't make this shit up!

***

I remember waiting for my sister to come off the plane in Fredericton. Someone poked my shoulder and a scratchy voice asked, "Do you know anywhere to get a taxi around here?"

Somewhat irritated, I turned around and saw my mother standing there! We both hooted and hugged. I'm sure my face registered a slight bit of horror, as I had no room for Mom AND Brenda at my place!

As fate would have it, Brenda piped up, "Oh, we booked a hotel, do you mind dropping us off?"

And so, we did. But we had no idea what we were in for.

***

The hotel Brenda had booked on the phone from Ontario, had seen better days. The green hotel sign was only half-lit. The hotel was dated and run down, and the lobby stunk of musty cigarettes. The burgundy striped carpet was worn from foot traffic and thousands of luggage wheels. A disheveled night clerk with a pen in his mouth greeted us. He mumbled, "Can I help you?" while his lips curled around the pen to keep it from falling out of his clenched teeth.

My sister glanced at me in disbelief.

After checking in and getting the keys, we climbed the stairs to the room, chatting about our plans for the next few weeks. Mom used the key to open the door, and she entered the room first, followed by Brenda, Gord (with the bags), and then me!

Mom stopped dead and hissed, "There are people in here, there are people in here!"

Her stopping so abruptly caused the four of us to collide like a set of bowling pins slammed by a bowling ball.

Hushed voices from the darkened room made us realize— there were indeed, "people in here"!

I gasped and slapped my hand across my mouth. There weren't just "people in here"—there were naked people in here. Doing things— in here!

We backed out fast, bumping into each other and our luggage. We couldn't get to the front desk fast enough!

The night clerk, pen still in his mouth, was in disbelief. "That can't possibly be."

Mom handed him the keys and said, "Well, you're welcome to go check, but I don't think the couple will be happy with a second interruption."

And then she said, "But I may have learned some new moves!"

Only once Mom and Brenda were settled in a new room, albeit in the basement of the hotel, did we allow ourselves to process what happened.

Everyone collapsed, laughing their asses off.

The incident became the highlight of our trip, and periodically one of us would spontaneously burst into giggles followed by a few snorts.

And the story didn't end there.

***

Years later, and on the opposite side of the country, I went for dinner with friends, Heather and Harry (names have been changed to protect the naked). My husband Gord was away fighting fires, and I was on maternity leave awaiting the birth of our first child. We began chatting about our most embarrassing moments.

I mentioned this wasn't MY embarrassing moment, but I told the crazy story about the couple we walked in on years ago during a cheap hotel stay in Fredericton. I proceeded to tell the whole encounter (night clerk – pen, included) moment by moment, and my friends paled and looked at each other in shock.

Recognition slowly spread across their faces. My friend Heather squeaked out, "That was us, you walked in on US! That was the first time we were in a hotel together. Our secret celebration!"

Through fits of laughter, my friends recounted their side of the story, describing their mortification because they'd been caught in such a compromising position by a group of strangers.

"And …my… dad… is… a… preacher!" gasped Heather.

Seriously, what are the chances?

Although we coined it an unforgettable moment, clearly it was now forgettable for Mom.

Aw, Sybil. I wish you could still remember it.

But I did tell my friends you'd said you'd learned a few new moves from them.

So that's got to count for something.

CHAPTER 4:

LOTS OF F-BOMBS AND DRUNK OBIT WRITERS

Ugh. It pours rain outside the airport. I feel it's following me across the country like a cloud of sadness. And my socks are still wet.

My brother, Brian, and I grab a taxi to pick up his truck and his daughter. We have a long, three-hour night drive ahead of us.

Brian drives and rubs his temples. We don't have any Tylenol for his splitting headache. I drag out a mini-roller from my purse and suggest some essential oil.

"Peppermint does the trick for me." I hand the small vial to his daughter Mason who is in the seat behind him. She leans forward and rolls it on both his temples and forehead. He instantly feels the iciness.

A few seconds later, he starts to sniff and tear up.

"What? Are you okay?" I ask. "I know it's tough, but it will be okay."

My brother yells, "What the fuck is this stuff? I can't fucking see! It's in my fucking eyes! My eyes are burning! I can't open my eyes! I can't fucking see! What the fuck?"

I lost count after the ninth F-bomb. I was laughing so hard that I clearly miss the potential danger of him driving blind on the 401! We can't even pull over as we're on the largest multi-lane highway in Ontario. I grab the wheel while he keeps swearing and we keep laughing.

And why is laughing in the midst of grief so weirdly satisfying?

I can't help but laugh and remember the first time I heard Mom drop the F-bomb.

***

"Oh, fuck!"

The words hung in the air for a moment like the stench of freshly sprayed skunk.

Who was that? It couldn't have been Mom. I put my book down and walked to the kitchen where the profanity was flying.

"I can't believe I did this to myself!"

And then she saw me.

Mom looked at me with wide eyes and apologized for swearing. She had a pained look—but it wasn't because she'd cursed. I looked down at the counter and realized her fingers were stuck in the beaters of the hand mixer. She'd been making her famous mayonnaise chocolate cake and the batter was all over her hand.

"Oh, my gawd, Mom! Did you use your fingers to wipe off the excess batter? You always told us to be …"

Mom interrupted, "Go get your father, dear!"

My mother had just said a word that was frowned upon in our home, a word I'd NEVER heard from her before.

I was sixteen. I dropped F-bombs all the time and so did my friends, but MY mom?

Never.

I ran upstairs to get Dad. He took one look at Mom and shook his head with a bit of a laugh muttering, "Oh, Sybil." Dad grabbed each beater, pulled them apart, and freed their grip on her fingers.

Mom had a dent in her fingers for the rest of the day. She was too embarrassed to share with us just how it happened.

But really.

"Oh, fuck," was a completely appropriate response to losing a battle with a hand mixer.

***

The rain keeps pounding on the truck windshield, but thankfully, Brian's eyes aren't streaming peppermint oil any longer. We're getting closer to Bracebridge.

Who'd ever think you'd want to hear your mother swear again?

Well, I do.

It's been so long since I've heard her voice, I now have trouble hearing her in my mind.

***

We check into our hotel; Brenda is meeting us here for dinner. I have just enough time to change out of my wet socks!

I nervously approach the restaurant entrance. Brian opens the door and follows after Mason and me.

I think, Okay. *Let's get this fucking over with.*

My heart races and my palms are clammy as I prepare to meet Brenda and her daughter for the first time in nearly ten years. I haven't seen her since our bitter falling out over a decade ago, a dispute that tore our family apart. But now with Mom's passing, I know it's time to put aside our differences and honour her together.

I scan the restaurant, and it doesn't take long to spot my short sister. Standing beside her, is my niece, Rachel. She's smiling. Wow. She's all grown up. The last time I saw her she was ten years old and missing a front tooth. Luckily for her, she didn't inherit her mom's short gene. She's now a head taller and just as beautiful.

Brenda's ash blonde hair is longer than I remember. Soft curls frame her pretty face. She looks great— Brenda is a hairstylist, and she always looks put together. The vanity in both of us shows when we give each other the "once over" comparing if one of us has gained more weight than the other over the years. The thought makes me smile. We truly are sisters.

It was at this moment I realize how much I've missed her.

Rachel walks toward us and hugs Mason and then me. I look back and Brenda's gaze meets mine. I walk over to her, and a tense silence hangs between us for a brief moment. The lines on her face have deepened over the years, as have mine. The sadness in her eyes mirrors my own. She hesitates for a moment before stepping into my outreached arms for a hug.

"Wine. Where is the wine?" I say, pulling away in search of a bottle while my brother and sister greet each other. My sister laughs and says, "I figured we'd need a bottle or two, I ordered some, and it's coming, don't worry."

Perhaps it's the wine, perhaps it's the sadness, but I know I have to start right then and there on Mom's obituary. I'm not prepared so I ask our server for a pen and a piece of paper.

Mom becomes the ice-breaker.

I ask my siblings if they want to add anything. My brother says a boilerplate template doesn't suit Mom; her obituary has to be different. My sister says Mom wasn't ordinary so she can't have an ordinary obituary AND it has to have something about her swimming to the buoy and back. They both agree our childhood nicknames should be included.

I start to write…

"It hurts me to admit it…but I, Mrs. Ron Hicks of Baysville, have passed away."

I want to write it in her words, to give Mom's voice back for one final time. To allow her to say goodbye.

I continue to write and scratch out words, write some more, taking a sip here and there of the fine red wine my sister has chosen. It's most definitely NOT Carlo Rossi from a box. A wine my mom often bought, buying for quantity not quality.

As the evening unfolds, the bottles of wine are uncorked one by one, and the deep red hues seem to match the emotions flowing at our table. Memories are shared: childhood adventures, family vacations, family fibs, and the quieter "oh shit" moments that defined our upbringing.

During dinner, we laugh more than we cry. As we begin to discuss the arrangements, a newfound sense of unity emerges. We laugh through more tears as we continue to reminisce about our childhood. So many memories flood back. It's what Sybil would have wanted — us finding solace in the stories that painted vivid memories of our childhood and of Mom's life.

Between sips, we interrupt each other with anecdotes and secret stories. Some I've never heard of before and some I don't want to be reminded of— like the time my eldest brother, Bob, told me I was adopted. I was eight and fell for it…for ten years.

The hours fly by and once the last wine bottle is almost dry, I've written a full page.

I take one last gulp of wine and say, "Okay, listen up!"

I share the hastily written obituary — Brian and Brenda both look at me with a few tears and go silent, and then they roar with laugher. My nieces exchange a look between them with raised eyebrows.

It could have been the wine or the sheer exhaustion of it all. But we howl at the table. We decide to run it past our younger brother who'll gauge if it's suitable or if we've just become drunk obit writers.

We call him. I read it out loud. He's silent, sucks in his breath, and says, "Uhm, I don't know about this," and exhales loudly.

We decide to call Dad. Dad has to be the one to okay it.

His reaction is similar to my youngest brother's.

Silence.

But he laughs heartily and says, "Run with it. I hope her eulogy and her service have the same sense of fun."

I hope you're there to see it, Sybil.

Because what a fucking night!

September 20, 1985

Dear Barb,

I hope this letter finds you well and still not too traumatized by your brother's creative storytelling skills. I am still flabbergasted about Bob telling you that you were adopted! The worst part? Your entire childhood and teen years you believed we were your adopted parents vs the real deal! I was so furious when you called, I just about had two cats and a kitten!

Honestly, I start sweating just thinking about it.

Let me reassure you that you are not adopted. I distinctly remember when you were born. Your father dropped me off at St. Jospeh's Brant. Yes, dropped me off—husbands weren't allowed in the delivery room back in those days. You arrived on December 27th, at 3:48 pm. Dr. Kellington was a wonderful man and our family doctor for years. He remembers your birth well — you were rather loud upon your arrival.

Trust me—I gave birth to you. I have the scars to prove it.

Anyway, just writing to say hello and let you know I miss you. It sounds like quite an adventure in Holland. Brenda said you don't sound like you anymore, she says you have an accent. I know she was happy you called her on her birthday yesterday.

I enjoy hearing about your new friends. Laura and Marca sound so sweet. Your adventure by bicycle to the Wham concert sounds like you made a lot of wonderful memories.

Biking to school each day, does it take you a long time? Those pouring rainy days must make the journey to school miserable.

I'm glad your studies are going great despite the language difference. I know you will do well regardless, dear.

In the meantime, if you ever have any questions about your adoption status —which rest assured does not exist—feel free to ask me. I am an open book and unlike your brother's stories, my tales are 100% fact-checked.

Love,

Mom

P.S. I am considering giving Bob an adoption certificate of his own for Christmas!

CHAPTER 5:

WILL MY REAL PARENTS PLEASE STAND UP?

I lay Mom's letter on the bedside table next to my coffee. Two cats and a kitten— makes me smile. Both Mom and my grandma said this phrase often over the years.

Last night at dinner, the traumatizing story of my adoption came up…I can laugh about it now. Bob, my eldest brother of six years, told me when I was eight years old that I was adopted. Yes, he was fourteen when he said it. He was a teenager but he was my big brother, I thought I could trust him. I remember the day he told me. I fell face-first on the couch, my legs sticking up at an awkward angle over the arm of the couch. I remember lifting my head off the couch long enough to yell at him, "At least they chose me – they were stuck with you!" and returned to my endless sobbing. I laid there and cried for so long, my legs were pins and needles when I finally stood to walk.

I don't know why I never asked my parents about it. I just assumed my ancient brother must be right.

Over the years as I grew older, I searched my parents' desk, bedroom dresser drawers, filing cabinets, and cupboards—trying to find proof of my birth or my adoption.

I found nothing. Not even baby photos.

It wasn't until I was eighteen, living in the Netherlands, that I discovered who my real parents were.

The Dutch government had an issue with my student visa that needed validation and I had to get a form from the Canadian embassy — the form stated, "birth parents" NOT "and/or guardians". Right there in black and white were the names: Ron Hicks and Sybil Hicks.

My hand flew to my mouth.

They WERE my parents!

***

When I heard Mom's voice on the other end of the phone, I started to sob. She was alarmed, "Are you okay?" When I could finally talk, I said, "You ARE my mom. You and Dad. You ARE my parents!"

"Of course, we are, what on earth are you talking about?"

"Bob told me I was adopted. He told me a long time ago!"

"What? When?"

"When I was about eight, Bob told me I was adopted. I've believed him and always thought I was adopted. I just came back from the Canadian embassy. My documents say you and Dad are my REAL parents."

"Of course, we are. You most certainly are NOT adopted. You need only to look in the mirror to know you are my daughter."

***

During the rest of our conversation, I explained how I learned how adopted children take on the characteristics of their adoptive parents and then tend to look like them. I said how I tried to find proof and found nothing, no baby pictures either. Her responses as to why there weren't any pictures or documents didn't truly matter. Something about them being tucked away where I hadn't looked, or about being the fourth child; she was so busy that not a lot of photos were taken. But when my younger brother, Bruce was born, and Mom almost died —there were tons of him being the last Hicks baby. All her words were like Charlie Brown's teacher— blah blah blah. I was still focused on the proof I'd found.

It only took ten years and 7839.11 km away from home to find it!

Before she hung up, I heard, "Robert Ronald Hicks, get down here right now!" I could tell by her voice that her teeth were clenched and her nostrils would be flaring.

What I wouldn't have given to be a fly on the wall when my mom confronted my brother.

Boy, he sure picked a bad day to visit Mom and Dad!

***

I carried that family fib with me for years.

One day while working in my home office, I must have been in my early thirties, I was listening to a Toronto radio station. The announcer invited listeners to call or write in and share family fibs that were passed down over the years.

I wrote in.

I shared the whole adoption story from start to finish.

I didn't know what became of my letter until my brother, Brian, called and told me he'd been driving on the 401 and heard the announcer read my letter. Apparently, driving while listening proved to be treacherous for Brian—he was laughing hysterically. He managed to find a spot to pull over safely and listened to the announcer read the rest of my letter.

When he'd finished reading, Brian said all he could think was, Mom is going to love this!

Aw, Sybil. You just can't make this shit up.

***

I glance at my watch. Time to head to the funeral home to see my adopted mother.

My one and only baby photo.

CHAPTER 6:
THE ARRANGEMENTS

My brother Brian knocks on my hotel room door. I'm ready and waiting.

Bob, Brian, Brenda, and I are going to the funeral home. Bruce will join us later in the week.

Reynolds Funeral Home was in Bracebridge forever. It's quiet, peaceful, and familiar. It wasn't my first time here, but this time is different— this time it's for my mom. It feels weird.

The funeral director greets us. His name is Bond. David Bond. A tall, kind-looking man with a genuine smile, and a professional attitude. I instantly like him. Mom is in good hands.

Introductions aside, and a chuckle about all our names beginning with the letter B, we start to chat about the particulars of Mom's service. We discuss details, sign papers, and are given the low down on moving forward.

David looks at all of us and asks gently, "Would you like to see your mom?"

***

An elevator rattles and stops on the other side of the wall; Mom has arrived. David invites us into a smaller room with low light. Mom's on a gurney draped in a rich burgundy velvet cloth. Hard to believe our once vibrant and full-of-life mother now lies so serenely. She looks peaceful. She looks like Mom, but oddly —not.

The four of us line up alongside Mom. Bob, me, Brenda, and Brian. I panic – *Maybe I shouldn't have agreed to see Mom this way, perhaps this was a mistake. Did I want this to be my last memory of seeing her for the very last time?*

Too late. Here I am peering over, taking her all in.

It is surreal.

I draw closer, then I spot her fingertips. They're stained with a peculiar shade of black. I start to giggle.

Earlier, I'd asked my sister to capture Mom's fingerprints for me as a keepsake or perhaps a tattoo. My whimsical idea turned into a messy experiment leaving traces of ink on almost all her fingers. I have trouble controlling my laughter. I point out Mom's hands to the others.

I snort.

We can't help but smile through tears at the absurdity of this moment. Funny how humour has its way of weaving strange threads through the fabric of reality at the worst possible moments.

I hear a subtle click. Bob, has reached over our mother's body to capture a photo of her blackened fingertips. It's a snapshot that will forever encapsulate our polarized emotions.

We try to suppress our laughter, but that makes it worse. We're choking, snorting, and bursting with laughter. We scramble out of the viewing room like rats fleeing a sinking ship and come face to face with the funeral director.

***

"So, David, you've just witnessed that this isn't an ordinary family."

He grins, "I gathered that, having read your mom's obituary."

***

Back in the front room of the funeral parlor, to confirm details of Mom's cremation, service, and other formalities — the question of her blackened fingers comes up.

Brenda glares at me in a huff.

"Barb, this is one of the most, if not THE, most stupid thing you've ever asked me to do! I sent Rachel to Staples to get an ink pad, the girl at the store had no idea what an ink pad was. The clerk asked Rachel what she wanted it for?"

Rachel said to her, "It's to take a fingerprint of my dead grandmother's finger."

Rachel said the salesperson screwed up her face as though she smelled stinky cheese, and responded slowly with, "Uhm, no, we don't have any of those!"

"Then I tried a black Sharpie! I couldn't get any of Mom's prints and NOW her fingers are all black. Permanently black!" she shrieks.

I think I'm going to pee my pants.

***

David roars with laughter after hearing the story.

"You know, Barb, we offer a service for capturing digital prints of your loved one's fingerprints. NO ink pads or Sharpies required."

"Well, I know that— NOW."

"Which fingerprint would you like to have digitalized?

I grin and blurt out, "This one!" Extending my middle finger and wiggling it in front of him.

I think for a quick moment he's taken aback, but then a burst of laughter erupts from him.

"We can certainly make that happen. Now, how to describe it on this form?" he says as he leans over his papers.

Brenda pipes up, "Just put: right hand, middle bird-flipping finger. She was always doing that to Dad!"

***

Can this get any crazier?

Aw, Sybil!

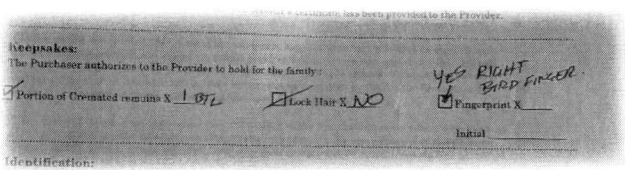

Funeral director's note on which finger to digitalize.

CHAPTER 7:
THE ORIGINAL SPELLING QUEEN

I realize I had to finish the damn eulogy. It's coming fast.

I look down at my paper, catch a spelling error, make the correction, and instantly think of Mom. She had an uncanny knack for spelling. Her words flowed effortlessly from her pen with her elegant handwriting, a style I've tried so hard to copy over the years.

***

"Sybil, how do you spell "conscientious?" Dad calls out to Mom from the roll-top desk in the living room.

"What?" Mom yells back from the kitchen. "What did you say?"

"Con-she-en- shush!" Dad hollers back. "How do you spell it?"

"C-o-n-s-c-i-e-n-t-i-o-u-s" Mom said back emphasizing each letter.

Hearing them, I giggle in my room at the top of the stairs– neither of them were willing to go to the other …yelling was easier.

"One more time but slower," Dad continues.

"C. O. N. S. C. I. E. N. T. I. O. U. S!" Mom said slowly, pausing between each letter.

"Thank you," Dad responded quietly.

"We need to get you a dictionary!"

"No, WE don't," Dad said. He waited for a beat and then added… "I have you."

A snort was heard from the kitchen.

***

It wasn't an accident Mom was a world-class speller. The woman inhaled books.

She was a voracious reader: stacks in the living room, stacks in the bathroom, and stacks by her bedside. (Much like the ones now stacked next to my side of the bed!) Mom's thirst for knowledge was evident in the variety of books she gathered.

Fiction from a variety of authors: Erma Bombeck, Peter Gzowski, and many Farley Mowat & Stephen Leacock editions. Jan Auel's *Clan of The Cave Bear.* James Herriot's hilarious UK vet adventures elicited several snorts from her within each chapter. The Thorn Birds by Colleen McCullough—she dragged that book everywhere. Mom told me once, "Everyone should read Ayn Rand's *When Atlas Shrugged.*"

I found a copy of it not too long ago…I guess I'll discover soon enough why everyone should read it.

As Alzheimer's took its toll on Mom, her voracious appetite for interaction with life, particularly reading, began to wane. Unfortunately, due to the deterioration of her cognitive function, Mom began a gradual withdrawal from her beloved world of words that had once been a source of joy and intellectual stimulation.

We witnessed her many times sitting on her chair lost in an open book—not in the story itself as she once had—but this time losing herself in the labyrinth of forgotten words and disordered thoughts.

***

"Hey, Mom, what are you reading?" Mom appeared to be halfway through a large hardcover novel.

She looked up, "Pardon?"

"Just want to know what you're reading?"

Mom tilted her head toward the book, "Oh, uhm, this one," she said lifting the book to show me.

The book was upside down.

"Is it good?"

Mom gazed at the book for a moment and then back toward me. Her eyes reflected a mix of confusion and fear. "Oh, yes, very interesting. I like the pictures. Very colorful."

I realized this must be quite a challenge for her now.

"That's wonderful, Mom. I bet the pictures tell quite a story. Anything else you want to share about it?"

Mom paused.

Had I pushed the conversation too far?

"Well, it's a bit jumbled, but—I like the colors. They make me happy."

It was at that moment I began to grasp the limitations Alzheimer's imposed on Mom. I cherished the moment and was grateful for the connection despite knowing this was just the beginning.

"Mom," I mentioned gently, "You have the book upside down."

"Oh, do I?" She looked down once again. "So, I have! Well, that's a new way to read, isn't it?" She closed her eyes, shook her head, and gave a genuine laugh followed by a snort.

Aw, Sybs.

***

I continue writing. It isn't easy getting lost in all the family memories, but then the words begin to flow. So many moments of spontaneous adventures, dinners around the twenty-one-foot table, renovations, parties, camping trips, ice skating, all the laughs with Aunt Mary and Uncle Ray and the rest of the Kosmacks, the shenanigans with our dear friends, the Foxes. Good grief, how can I keep her eulogy short?

***

Music books, horticultural books, biographies and glossy-paged coffee table books, and an impressive eclectic array of recipe books always lay scattered around my parents' home.

Mom's copy of *Better Homes and Gardens*, with the signature red gingham cover, was propped against the ceramic wash basin on a little oak washstand in the kitchen. Leaning next to it was her cherished *The Fannie Farmer Cookbook.* On the inside cover, Mom had sketched a map of where the septic system was buried. And she did this years before Alzheimer's. Why she felt Fannie Farmer should hold the secret to the septic system is beyond me. I'm surprised Mom didn't draw it on the pea soup page!

My sister gave the book to me after Mom had passed. Seeing her handwriting on the inside of the book takes me right back to my childhood kitchen and I smile at the memory.

Reading her cookbooks gives me a strangely beautiful comfort—even if I don't cook a thing from them.

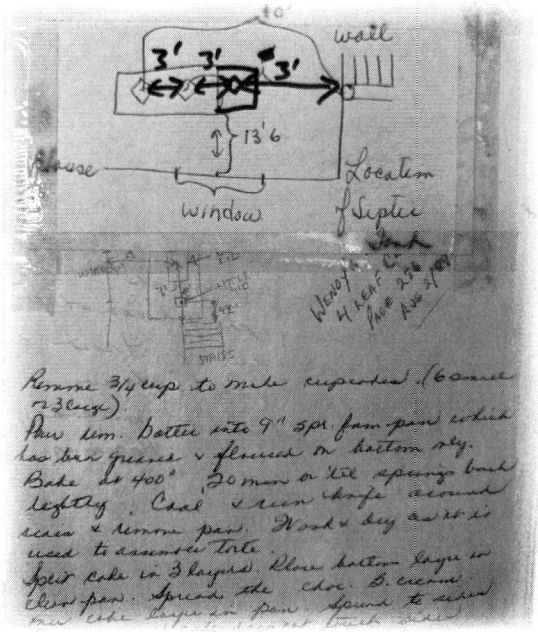

Mom's septic tank drawing.

***

One day while reading her Fannie Farmer Cookbook, the mystery of the "thin pancakes" that plagued my parents' marriage for years, was solved.

Often Fridays were meatless, although I'm not sure why. Perhaps the expense of meat? It certainly didn't have a religious reason behind it. So rather than a meat dish Mom would make pancakes.

"I wish you could make pancakes like my mom used to!" Dad whined. "Mom's pancakes were much, much thinner than these!"

Friday after Friday, Mom tried new recipes and each pancake was met with the same complaint from Dad, "Not thin enough!"

As a result of Mom's love of reading, she discovered a recipe from her Fannie Farmer's Cookbook.

"1 cup flour, 4 eggs, ¼ cup water, 2 Tbsp sugar…"

"This sounds like a pancake but…mmm? I wonder?" Mom pondered.

That Friday, Mom produced the pancakes from this recipe, and they turned out paper-thin.

"Finally, you know how to make pancakes like my mom!" Dad exclaimed.

"Well, had you asked for "CREPES" you could have eaten these years ago. How do you spell horse's ass??"

***

I snort at the memory.

I know Mom's recipe by heart and these "thin pancakes" are now a staple in our house too.

I should have put her pancake recipe in the obit—hundreds of thousands of people could be eating them right now! (And yes, I'd check my spelling!)

The Fannie Farmer Cookbook.

CHAPTER 8:
WHO ELSE HAS A
RENAISSANCE MOTHER?

Mom's brilliance extended far beyond the realm of intellect. A symphony of creativity if you will. She played the piano with a deftness that channeled her very soul into the keys. She had particularly quick fingers for *Hello Dolly* and *Flight* of the *Bumble Bee.*

Even when Mom lived in the nursing home, on the rare occasion when her neurons were firing on point, she'd pound out a song on the piano in the common room. The moment the last note struck the keyboard, Mom sat back in silence, hands in her lap, and she'd ask out loud to no one in particular,

"What am I doing here, I don't know how to play the piano?" [1]

She'd get up and wander down the hall.

She was fired up, but her neurons weren't. [2]

***

When I was a teen, Mom and I took painting lessons from a famous local artist, Richard Karon. Mom had artistic talent—barrels of it. Me? Not so much. Every smear of paint, palette knife swipe, or brush stroke was a testament to her unique talent and eye for color.

---

1 Listening to and performing music reactivates areas of the brain associated with memory, reasoning, speech, emotion, and reward. Music doesn't just help us retrieve stored memories; it also helps us lay down new memories. Music may reduce agitation and improve behavioral issues that are common in the middle stages of the disease. Even in the late stages of Alzheimer's, a person may be able to tap a beat or sing lyrics to a song from childhood. (Harvard Health 2015)

2 In Alzheimer's disease, as neurons are injured and die throughout the brain, connections between networks of neurons may break down, and many brain regions begin to shrink. By the final stages of Alzheimer's, this process—called brain atrophy—is widespread, causing significant loss of brain volume. (National Institute on Aging 2023)

And her talents didn't stop there. She was a Renaissance woman.

Mom's textile skill was demonstrated by each seam she sewed into countless costumes, skirts, pants, bathing suits, coats, and jackets. Oh, and the many polyester school outfits she made us wear. I have proof — a photo of my sister and me in these snazzy blue polyester gems. She even had a little sewing business called "Sybil's Sewing Cellar."

Mom taught the interested ladies of Baysville how to create ten-cent t-shirts; the art of adding a zipper, and how to create rolled ruffle hems at home in our basement. At one point, at every church function or local event, families arrived wearing their ten-cent t-shirts and the women showed off their ruffled hems!

***

Mom's talents weren't confined to the tangible. She had a sharp wit, and one-liners, and was often up for practical jokes or pies in the face. Mainly pies in the face!

Usually, the unassuming victim would be invited for dinner, or over for coffee and pie. And Mom with her impeccable timing and element of surprise was able to pull off another pie in the face!

More often than not, it landed in the face of a family member, or a friend who'd made a smart-ass comment. No one ever got upset with Mom, on the contrary, I think they felt honored to be among the chosen few.

Once I added the pies up. It came to over twenty-five pies! I'm pretty sure I missed a bunch. Sybs averaged about two pie throws in the face per year before she dove into the world of Alzheimer's —which is like the ultimate pie-in-the-face, don't you think?

She didn't deserve that one, Universe.

Sometimes Mom would have an assortment of pies on the table, on the dock, or even when we went camping. Some were cream pies, and the others were fruit pies, or occasionally her impossible pie would appear on the table.[3]

As her children, we knew someone that night was going to end up with pie in their eyes!

Strangely, no one ever got mad at her. It all ended in belly laughs and people rolling on the ground laughing or trying to get the whipped cream off their eyelashes. No wonder there weren't any pictures taken!

---

3 She was so proud of that pie, but it was rather disgusting. It was a pie that made its own crust and was supposed to taste like coconut cream pie. I called it the Pie of Disappointment. Perhaps that's why I'm not a fan of coconut pie. Brenda says it was called impossible pie because it was an impossible pie to eat.

***

I was driving with Mom to town one day and a huge bug hit the windshield leaving a gooey neon splat.

In a serious tone, Mom asked, "Do you know the last thing that went through that bug's mind?"

"Uhm, no… what?"

"His ass."

"Mom, that's not even remotely funny," I said.

"I bet he doesn't have the guts to do that again!"

I rolled my eyes.

Mom snorted.

***

All these little things truly set her apart – including her infectious laughter punctuated with a snort at the end, which was a unique and endearing quirk.

I may not have a green thumb, play the piano, or make hanging macrame lamps the size of a barn, but I do have her snort.

It reminds me I'm not adopted.

CHAPTER 9:

TWO DAYS TO GO AND I'M FREAKING OUT

I have two days to finish Mom's eulogy. It's getting more difficult to write. The memories are particularly draining—it's such an emotional rollercoaster.

How the hell did my brilliant, hilarious, and kind Mom end up pulling the freaking Alzheimer's wild card from the deck of life? I guess we play what we're given—and she did for a long, long time. No different than Gordon and me, rolling the genetic dice and having our youngest child born with Down

Syndrome.[4] A roll I wouldn't take back for a million tries. Clark is so precious. We love and adore him like we do all our children.

Clark and Mom had quite a connection—more than just a gramma to a grandchild (the natural allies kind of thing)—but a connection on a cellular level. Not long after Mom was diagnosed, I learned people with Down syndrome are more likely to develop Alzheimer's disease than a typical person.[5]

---

4 Down syndrome is a condition in which a person has an extra chromosome. It is named after John Langdon Down, the British physician who described the syndrome for the first time in 1866. Chromosomes are small "packages" of genes in the body. They determine how a baby's body forms and functions as it grows during pregnancy and after birth. Typically, a baby is born with 46 chromosomes. Babies with Down syndrome have an extra copy of one of these chromosomes, chromosome 21. A medical term for having an extra copy of a chromosome is 'trisomy.' Down syndrome is also referred to as Trisomy 21. This extra copy changes how the baby's body and brain develop, which can cause both mental and physical challenges for the baby. (CDC Centers for Disease Control and Prevention.)

5 Approximately 40–80% of persons with Down syndrome (DS) develop Alzheimer's disease (AD)—like dementia by the fifth to sixth decade of life (NIH National Library of Medicine.) I pray my sweet boy never has to deal with this crap.

Mom and Clark at the piano.

We meet with Reverend M. Barnes today to go over Mom's service plan. I want to keep writing as much as I can before then.

Reading Mom's letters helps. So, I've pulled another letter from the stash I brought with me.

Am I a bad person to say I'd rather eat a bucket of popcorn in bed and watch a movie instead of preparing a eulogy for my mother?

This is fucking hard.

August 16, 1989

Dear Barb,

I am sure you are well despite the studying and shenanigans of university life. I remember those times, believe it or not! Yes, I was young once too!

I have tried the dorm phone, but someone always answers, goes off to look for you and never comes back. So, call me when you get a chance.

I am eager to hear all about your experiences and the wonderful practicum you will be doing. Remember, no matter how challenging it gets, I have every faith in your abilities.

Speaking of challenges, here's some news I want to share with you! Remember how Dad quit smoking cold turkey back in the summertime? He did well at that time, and I did not. Well, guess what? Your stubborn old mother has finally decided to follow in his footsteps! Yes, after forty long years of trying to kick the habit.

Let me tell you, it has been quite an adventure so far. Unlike your father who seemed to have superhuman willpower (or superhuman stubbornness), I'm struggling with it a bit. In the summer on my first attempt to quit, I would go to the boathouse to find any butts in old ashtrays! I have no shame.

Oh, the stories I could tell you about my recent attempts to find old cigarette butts! I have rummaged through every purse, bag, and jacket I have owned in the past decade, just to see if I've missed even the smallest butt. You wouldn't believe the odd looks I've received from your father while performing my desperate searches!

He asked me, "Do you really want to smoke a cigarette butt from 1980?

But then, success! I found a very short cigarette, mostly the filter, but I tried to light it anyways and almost burnt my fingers. It was so small! Can you imagine how desperate I was? Well, did I ever laugh. Of course, my laugh was followed by a few snorts which led your father to find me. Your father just shook his head and said, "Aba baba boo," and then we laughed all over again.

Can you just picture me doing this? Who knew quitting could lead to such ridiculous adventures. I hope this made you laugh.

However, my pursuit of a final smoke has led me to discover a few unusual things: a lollipop from an old trip to Nel's Candy shop with a bus full of kids on the last day of school, a receipt from a restaurant I don't recall ever visiting, an old pair of pearl earrings, an almost empty lipstick and an old Lions Club pin from Huntsville. Now wasn't that a find?

Anyway, enough about my shenanigans. Tell me what's happening at UNB. How are classes? How are Jennifer, Joe, and the Great Swami?

That's all for now, sweetie.

Love,

Mom

CHAPTER 10:

FLYING HIGH WITH MOM AND MEETING THE GOOD REVEREND

I push my notes away for a minute to take a break from writing the eulogy. I'm close to finishing it, but I know the reverend is coming over soon which adds even more pressure to get it right.

I read Mom's letter again which makes me laugh. For a woman so bright, poised, and intelligent? Crazy antics followed her. I never followed her cigarette habit—I did, however, try smoking one of those green mosquito coils we used down on the dock each summer. I darn near passed out trying to inhale the solid chemical-packed coil. But we won't talk about that right now.

One fall, Dad needed a break from caregiving. I suggested to Dad that I fly to Ontario and bring Mom back to Peace River with me. I didn't know when I offered, just how far along Mom was in her Alzheimer's diagnosis.

***

I hugged Dad goodbye. "Don't worry, I'll take good care of her."

He leaned over to give Mom a hug and a kiss. "Right, bye."

Mom and I continued to the airport check-in desk. Her once long strides were now short deliberate steps. We watched our bags disappear on the conveyor belt. As we reached the security gates, I helped Mom remove her jacket and showed her where to place the carry-on in the bin.

"Mom, you wait here, and I'll go first." I made it through— without setting off alarms —that was a first!

I turned to look at Mom and waved her toward me. I heard the security guard state louder, "Next!" He waved Mom forward. Her eyes opened wider. I stepped toward the uniformed man, "That's my mom. She has dementia." I was about to call Mom when he told me to step back. I waved at Mom to come toward me. She stepped through the metal detector and a loud buzz went off. Mom stepped back in fear. Traveling was not new to Mom, but traveling with Alzheimer's was.

"Ma'am, step forward again and come through."

I felt so helpless. *What was I thinking —bringing her home by myself? Why did I go through the machine first?*

Mom stepped forward and I waved to keep her moving forward. This time she walked through.

The metal detector sounded again, and Mom covered her ears with her hands.

"Extend your arms, Ma'am." Demonstrating what he wanted Mom to do.

Mom kept her hands on her ears.

I looked at the other security personnel behind the plexiglass. I spotted an older woman who was watching this scene unfold.

"My Mom has Alzheimer's. She has a titanium hip and that's what made the machine buzz." My voice was an octave louder than normal.

The woman came around to my side. "Do you have any medical papers stating she has an artificial hip?"

"No, I didn't know she would need one. If you want to feel her hip you can feel the indentation—go ahead."

She stepped forward and whispered a few words to the younger security guard.

I saw her speak to Mom. Mom responded by lowering her hands. The woman reached out and touched one hip and then the other. She turned and nodded toward me and guided Mom to the bins. She pointed to a black bag on the belt and asked if it was Mom's.

"Yes," I said.

"Well then, let's have a look, shall we?" She smiled at Mom.

Out of Mom's bag, she pulled a solid old pewter jewelry box.

"Mind if I open this?"

I nodded my agreement.

Inside, Mom's jewelry was a tangled mess: necklaces, several rings, and a broken brooch.

"Okay, no problem. But I have to keep these." She held up a pair of elegant antique sewing scissors with a stork design and a mini-corkscrew wine opener.

I laughed, "Okay, she drinks the boxed wines now, anyway."

The woman smiled and said, "Okay Sybil, you're good to go now. Have a good flight." She handed Mom her boarding pass.

The younger security guard had wandered over and said, "Yes, have a good flight."

As we walked away Mom leaned toward me, "Asshole!" she muttered.

Pretty sure I heard the older woman chuckle.

***

Boarding the plane brought a mix of relief and apprehension on my part. We were seated close to the front. Mom by the window and me on the aisle. Mom, the once confident traveler, was now a confused passenger.

The confined space, the roar of the engines, and the intermittent announcements by the flight crew were a sensory overload for Mom. Amidst the turbulence of the flight and the once-familiar sounds of the cabin, her head darted like a curious bird—trying to make sense of the unexpected sounds surrounding her. I took her hand and tried to distract her with a bit of chit-chat. I told her about the kids and the acreage. But a sudden announcement, or the click of a seatbelt, or another passenger walking by prompted her to look in that direction. I saw lines on her forehead deepening with each startle—she felt vulnerable and afraid.

The guilt gnawed at me as I questioned whether this journey was a mistake. I longed for the days when she navigated airports with ease, and I didn't have to face this terrifying, disoriented version of my mom. The vibrant woman who had raised me, and guided me through teenage challenges; when I became a new mother, and other countless shared memories—was gone. Her once insightful conversations and intelligent soapbox lectures are replaced with fragmented sentences and vacant stares. We'd just started our journey and in a few short hours, I now see the true damage of Alzheimer's disease. It fucking hurt.

I felt like such a shit for doing this to her.

The gentle touch on Mom's shoulder by the flight attendant in an attempt to offer assistance was met with a confused look from Mom. The flight attendant seemed attuned to what was happening. She smiled, and offered Mom a glass of water or a soft drink.

"Ginger ale…please."

"Certainly."

Mom was happy with the ginger ale but became angry shortly after.

"What am I doing here? I want off. Where are we going? Where is Ron?"

She kept taking off her seat belt and trying to stand up. I was embarrassed—like when a child has a temper tantrum in the store and other shoppers look on with judgment. Then I became angry. Can't people just see the obvious?

"Here, Mom. Try this. It'll make you feel better." I shamelessly gave her a piece of chocolate and a chewable Gravol. She'd developed quite a sweet tooth over the years and was happy to accept it. Combined with the hum of the plane and twenty minutes of the Gravol being on board —Mom fell asleep for the rest of the flight.

I didn't fall asleep. I was contemplating my new life as a drug dealer.

***

"Are you almost done?" Brenda calls from the kitchen.

I'm on her living room couch, into my third coffee, and close to finishing the eulogy.

"Yeah, getting there. Why?"

"Reverend Barnes will be here soon."

"Where did you find him, again?"

"I went to a few funerals. He seemed like a good guy. I think Mom would like him."

***

Brenda greets Reverend Barnes at the front door and shows him into the living room. A figure of wisdom appears with distinguished white hair and a bushy beard. His eyes, knowing and compassionate, speak volumes about the solace he's offered to others in their grief. He has a slight stoop, and he immediately offers his hand with his condolences, his kind and genuine smile instantly puts me at ease.

Despite not knowing Mom, the reverend has taken time to meet with those who did know Mom. He reached out to friends, family, and anyone who could share insights into Mom's personality, values, and the impact she had on those around her.

When he speaks, his voice is soothing and melodic, and it resonates with calm authority. As I listen, his voice seems familiar. Each word is carefully enunciated—he sounds like someone I'd heard before. After a few minutes, it hits me—Stuart McLean, the late author and presenter of CBC Radio's Vinyl Cafe! The reverend speaks much like Stuart telling one of his heartfelt stories on the radio. Another reason this man is a good choice for Mom's service—she loved Stuart McLean.

During our meeting we share many stories and ideas that could be included in her service, however, many of them are already in my eulogy. He shows empathy and understanding and offers, "I'll follow your lead, Barbara. I'll create a summary that captures the essence of your mom's life and incorporate what I've learned from the others."

His genuine effort to understand Mom shows his dedication to help us create a meaningful tribute to her life. He is the real deal. Judging by the twinkle in his eyes when he speaks with us and listening to our Sybil stories, I know Mom would approve.

I don't think she'd call him an asshole.

CHAPTER 11:

THEY MIGHT HAVE PASSED A VERY PLEASANT EVENING HAD SHIT NOT GOTTEN REAL

Mom was unparalleled as a mother. She was a nurturing force with an innate ability to care for her family and friends in daily life and those in their most vulnerable moments. It's what made her an incredible emergency room nurse for fifteen years. And even after she quit nursing—she put her nursing skills to the test more times than I can count. Whether it was getting hooks and lures out of fishermen's legs and faces, fixing our childhood booboos, helping our favourite cousin Barry after he'd had an incident involving a skill saw and his thigh, or other serious injuries.

She also stepped up to help strangers in distress many times over the years.

One cold winter night in 1979, my middle-aged mother helped save a snowmobiler who'd fallen through the ice on the lake in front of our house.

Get ready. This story is like a TV movie.

***

"Ron, look! Someone's out on the ice! It's too thin—they are heading toward the open narrows!"

My friend Betty and I were upstairs in my room and had come downstairs after hearing Mom yell.

Dad started flicking the exterior floodlights on and off trying to warn the snowmobilers.

"I'm headed down to the dock!" Mom yelled as she threw on her winter coat and snowmobile boots. Mom went into nurse mode and barked orders as though she was back in the emergency room.

"Ron build a big fire, and get some towels and blankets ready!"

***

Yes—Mom went down to the dock, not Dad. Why? Mom knew Dad's incredible fear of the water.

I think they also both knew if medical attention was required, it should be Mom down there.

Dad stopped flicking the lights for fear of drawing the snowmobilers closer. He immediately started a fire in our large stone fireplace.

My friend and I pressed our faces to the window —trying to see any movement or lights in the dark.

After what seemed like an eternity, we saw Mom and some men who were half dragging and half carrying something.

OMG! It was a body!

I turned to my friend, "Betty, do you think the guy is…dead?

***

Mom and the others burst through the door. They held a soaking wet, frozen, and barely shivering man and laid him in front of the fire Dad had built earlier. Mom reverted to her nursing skills and the orders began again:

"Ron, call the ambulance!"

"Already called!" Dad answered.

"We need to take all his wet clothes off, NOW!"

"Ron, get the heating pad from the long bathroom cupboard!"

"Barb, run to the end of the road to meet the ambulance!"

"Ron," she barked louder so he could hear her at the top of the stairs, "Get the featherdown quilt from the hope chest in the upstairs living room!"

While she gave orders, she carefully took off the man's soaked clothes and started warming his arms and legs with towels to bring back his circulation. I knew she was worried about hypothermia[6] setting in.

**

---

6 Hypothermia is a medical emergency that occurs when your body loses heat faster than it can produce heat, causing a dangerously low body temperature. Normal body temperature is around 98.6 F (37 C). Hypothermia (hi-poe-THUR-me-uh) occurs as your body temperature falls below 95 F (35 C). When your body temperature drops, your heart, nervous system, and other organs can't work normally. Left untreated, hypothermia can lead to complete failure of your heart and respiratory system and eventually to death. Hypothermia is often caused by exposure to cold weather or immersion in cold water. Primary treatments for hypothermia are methods to warm the body back to a normal temperature. (Mayo Clinic 2023)

Betty and I ran about three hundred meters to the end of the road. We were out of breath from running the whole way, combined with fear of what we'd just witnessed. We reached the crest of the last hill and began our wait. It was a long twenty minutes before we heard the wail of the ambulance. It was freezing cold, but we didn't complain…we weren't that frozen guy inside the house.

We saw the ambulance lights and started jumping and waving our arms frantically at them.

The ambulance turned toward us, and the driver shouted, "Where to?"

Betty yelled, "To the end of the road, right to the end of the road!"

By the time we reached the house, the paramedics were closing the doors and heading to the hospital.

***

When we burst into the house, panting, we looked at Mom expectantly.

"He'll be all right girls, don't worry!" she said.

Even with her reassurance — we worried.

***

The local radio station was eager to broadcast the heroic rescue, and they focused on the sensational side of the story. They interviewed Mom a few days later.

The announcer said, "42-year-old Sybil Hicks from Baysville Ontario helped rescue a snowmobiler from the icy waters of Lake of Bays over the weekend."

"My husband and I saw what was happening. A snowmobiler was out on the ice. The ice was much too thin in the narrows to hold a snowmobiler. I knew he was in trouble. My husband tried flicking the exterior lights as a warning. But we were worried the person might think WE needed help. We were too late. The snowmobiler unknowingly ventured into open water. The headlight tilted skyward as the back end of the snowmobile sank with the rider—I knew he was in big trouble. I headed toward the lake and went out onto our neighbor's dock to help bring the gentleman to safety. It was quite an ordeal. He's a lucky man."

***

The media's selective reporting omitted the crucial detail that this daring rescuer wasn't just a courageous soul, but a skilled emergency room nurse who understood the urgency of immediately, yet carefully, warming the victim.

When they aired the interview, the narrative took an unexpected turn. The snippet they chose to highlight seemed to end with Mom saying,

"We got him in the house in front of the fire and I got him naked."

***

While researching the accident details for this book, I discovered "episodic memories".[7] Episodic memory refers to the experiences that make up our lives. It represents our conscious recollection of the past, the type of memory we use when we mentally travel backward in time, as in recalling a favourite book or a summer on the lake, a first kiss, or as in this story, a heroic rescue.

When I reached out to friends and family who may have known about this rescue and could offer me more details, I discovered each person had a different perspective and experience of the event.

I made a plea on Facebook, asking for anyone who may have a news clip or information regarding the time Mom saved Don Rawding's life. I knew it was a long shot, but I believed in the power of positive

7 Seamon, John. Memory & Movies What Films Can Teach Us About Memory. MIT Press, 2015

social media. My childhood friend, Judy, re-posted my request for help on the Lake of Bays Through the Years Facebook page, and low and behold—help was found.

Heather, a friend from high school reached out to her cousin, Andy McEachern. Andy was a friend of Don Rawding[8] and a fellow snowmobiler who was also on the ice that dreadful evening.

Andy, a kind gentleman, was happy to share his memories of that traumatic cold night. As he spoke, I realized his memory of that night was significantly different than mine, but both are true recollections. I could hear in his voice how the chilling event of 1979 influenced him even now.

***

"A few buddies and I including, Don Rawding and his brothers Ron and Rod and a cousin, Charles, were snowmobiling out on the Lake of Bays one night. We got turned around with our directions and instead of turning towards Dorset, we were heading to Baysville. Heading to open water.

---

8 At the time of writing, I couldn't locate Don Rawding for an interview. If you're reading this now, Don—I hope we can connect. For the record, I never saw you naked.

I was the lead snowmobiler and noticed the Dorset Tower and realized we were going the wrong way. Some of the guys had faster snowmobiles and sped off past us and went out ahead. Charles and I turned to correct our course. We stopped our snowmobiles to wait for them. That's when we saw the fog and knew there was open water and some of the snowmobilers were headed right for it.

We saw mass confusion with lights and all. We couldn't see everything that was happening, but we knew Don drove off the ice into open water.

Ron and Rod, Don's brothers, had noticed the open water and started snowmobiling along the shoreline.

Typically, there are only cottages around the lake in the winter and most everything is put away for the winter. However, Ron jumped off his snowmobile after spotting a canoe leaning against a shed.

It was close to the open water; he threw the canoe in the water and both brothers jumped in and paddled with their hands towards Don. One of the other fellas had found an aluminum boat. Don had been in the water for at least five minutes already. Don had somehow managed to take his helmet off when he first hit the water. The snowmobile had sunk, with good reason—it weighed around six hundred pounds! Don was in open water keeping himself up—barely. He was wearing a skidoo suit and winter boots that weighed a ton once they were wet.

With Ron and Rod paddling with their hands, they reached Don just as he was going down. Ron took off his helmet and boots, he was ready to jump in after him —but reasonable heads prevailed. Instead, Ron grabbed Don by the hair and held on. They took off his scarf and put it under his arms and were able to keep him from going under.

They managed to get him into the aluminum boat. Now, Don weighed about 220-lbs. His water-soaked snowmobile suit and boots would have added another hundred pounds, easily. I don't know how they did it. They maneuvered the boat toward your mom who was on the dock. I think it was Kelk's dock.

It took all of them to bring him up to your parents' home. Your dad had a fire waiting and that's where your mom got Don undressed and tried to help him. He wasn't talking and was already pretty much comatose. His hands were already frozen and white.

Don was taken to the hospital and seemed to be okay because we were able to pick him up at four in the morning. I know Don had trouble sleeping for the next while, each time he closed his eyes he would see water. His hands bothered him long after whenever they got cold. He told us later he didn't remember anything until they were almost halfway to the Bracebridge hospital.

A few days later, Friday I think, a bunch of us went back to retrieve his snowmobile. With a couple of meat hooks, we were able to pull it out. We had it started in about twenty minutes.

If your parents weren't home, particularly your mom, it would have been a different story altogether."

***

Not long after the accident, the Rawding family arrived and gave Mom and Dad a plaque, thanking them for saving Don's life. The other men who were involved in Don's rescue were also given plaques. All were gratefully given and all were humbly received.

And they didn't add anything on Mom's plaque about Don being naked.

We still have the plaque. Keeping it reminds us how Mom and Dad didn't hesitate to reach out to help a stranger. Seeing the plaque creates a tangible reminder of the heroics of that night by our mother.

I couldn't be prouder.

Once again, Mom, you showed us—you're a legend.

Too bad you couldn't remember this story for the last eighteen years of your life.

A decline in the ability to retrieve this kind of memory is among the first signs of Alzheimer's disease.

Sybs—we had no idea.

Plaque of thanks.

July 1982

Hi Sweetie,

I hope this letter finds you well. I feel bad you must stay in Fredericton for a bit this summer, the dock and water have been so warm and refreshing.

Speaking of the dock I have a funny story to tell you about a recent incident I had the other day. I took the rowboat out for a little ride to the sandbar, the sun was shining, and the water was so calm. Well, when I came back, I hit the shoreline and because my seat was wet, I slid to the floor of the boat.

I wish you could have seen my comical disaster—there I was, my bum on the bottom of the boat and my legs bent with my feet against the seat ahead of me. My life jacket protected my back against the seat behind me. But I could not budge! I was wedged in there like a sardine. And with my bum being so heavy, I struggled to try to get out of the boat.

Your father was on the dock watching and I couldn't help but burst into fits of giggles— I must admit there might have been a little more laughter added by the amusing (and embarrassing) sounds that accompanied my efforts—a combination of grunts, turns and yes, some unintentional farting. It was a moment of sheer vulnerability, and I couldn't help myself. I do not like middle age.

To keep this letter short, I will let you know I managed to get myself back onto the seat and then roll into the water. It felt so cool after my struggle.

As I write this, I can't help thinking about the time I was stuck in the bathtub, and you came to my rescue with the kitchen spatula! But I don't think you want to be reminded of that!

So, my dear, I hope this letter brings a smile to your face. Life's adventures may not always go as planned, but there's always room for laughter with a good old rowboat escapade.

Love,

Mom

Mom is stuck in the boat!

CHAPTER 12:

YOU CAN'T MAKE THIS SHIT UP

Reverend Barnes left a few hours ago. The time was well spent. I like this man. I think Mom would like him too!

I giggle after reading Mom's letter about the rowboat incident and my thoughts immediately raced back in time to the moment I was beckoned to help Mom out of yet another sticky situation.

***

I was in the kitchen making Mom's famous Miracle Whip chocolate cake. As I mixed the batter,

I thought I heard someone calling my name. Had I imagined it? One more time only much louder this time—"BARBARA!"

Uh, oh, my full name—what did I do now?

I put down the whisk and followed the sound. It was Mom. I went upstairs, the door to the long bathroom was closed, and behind it, came Mom's call for help. I tried to open the door, but it was locked.

"Mom, what's going on? Are you okay?"

"Just come in, I will explain when you come in!"

Before I could enter, I had to search for something that would fit inside to release the lock. I found a Bic pen, pulled out the refill, slid it into the hole, and gave a little push until I heard the click.

Whew!

I entered the bathroom not sure what to expect. I peered toward the short pony wall that separated the toilet and the bathtub, I couldn't see Mom, but I heard her. She was giggling now.

I walked a bit further. She was naked in the tub, on her back, bubbles almost gone— hiding nothing. Her head was at an awkward angle, her eyes closed, and her face scrunched from laughing.

"Uhm, Mom. What is going on?"

Mom laughed harder and a toot escaped causing bubbling sounds beneath the water, which in turn caused her to laugh harder and more sounds escaping.

"Mom! What the heck?"

When she finally caught her breath and in between snorts, I managed to get the story. But the more she spoke, the harder it became to suppress my laughter.

Mom had somehow managed to create the perfect suction with the bottom of the bathtub and her back! Attempts to free herself had proven futile. She was stuck as if she had octopus suckers on her back.

It was a moment of both confusion and amusement, and I burst out laughing!

"So, can you help me, please?"

"Mom, it looks like I'm in a power position here!"

She laughed and said, "Hurry up, I'm getting cold!"

Draining the tub wouldn't release the suction, I had to think of something and fast!

I ran back down to the kitchen and looked around for something to break the seal. A BBQ probe? Bad idea. A turkey baster? Bad idea. A corkscrew? REALLY bad idea. Finally, I grabbed the spatula I was using for the cake!

Back in the bathroom, I slid the spatula down the side and under her back, breaking the seal that held her captive. An odd noise punctuated under the water.

"THAT wasn't me!" Mom blurted.

Laughter echoed in the bathroom as we shared this moment of lighthearted absurdity. The ordeal wasn't without its awkward moments, but the hilarity of it all was first and foremost.

To this day, every time I reach for a spatula, I smile remembering the day that little kitchen utensil saved my mother's ass.

The naked part though, I wish I could unsee.

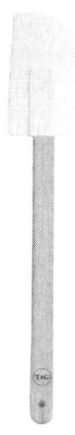

August 1983

Dear Barb,

Well, your father and I are in the middle of renovating the house in Bracebridge. I have been stripping and painting. (Just to be clear, stripping the paint off the window frames.) Ha Ha.

What a big job! There must be nine layers of paint. A few colors were hideous, no wonder they painted over them. Some of the windows were painted shut and I had to pry them open! I even broke a little screwdriver on one. I have been here for weeks. It has been extremely hot lately and very stuffy in the house and so with the windows finally open, I get a nice cross breeze.

We pulled up the shag carpets, they were so filthy. Low-and-behold, there was hardwood underneath. It is going to be lovely.

I have had the local radio station on, and every hour, on the top of the hour they have played, "A Rhinestone Cowboy." Every hour. I used to like Glen Campbell. I grit my teeth every time it comes on now. I finally got to the point where I turned the damn thing off. I'm so sick of that song I could vomit! I would rather listen to static.

Anyway, enough of that. I'm heading into town now — in my painting clothes and ready to go. But I just wanted to give you an update on our house project before I leave. I'll mail this on my way to town.

I hope you are having fun and working hard.

Love,

Mom

CHAPTER 13:

THE TORMENT
OF THE RHINESTONE COWBOY

Mom's letters are such a comfort. I'm so glad I brought them with me. Reading them allows me to hear her voice —and her snorts.

This letter made me laugh out loud! It's been years since I've thought about the house Mom and Dad renovated to flip. But I've often thought of her hatred for the Rhinestone Cowboy song after she heard it a million times during the renovations.

It reminds me of when my brother Brian and I experimented with the power of music on Mom.

One fall, Brian and I visited Mom at The Pines. It was during her later stages of the disease—she was no longer speaking, or walking—for the most part, she was completely dependent on her caregivers.

***

When Brian and I entered her room, Mom was in her customized wheelchair. She sat at a slight recline and was covered by a blanket. Her hair was a mess and she needed a good shampoo. Mom was rigid and her eyes were vacant, hollow—not drugged up as we'd sometimes witnessed on earlier visits—just empty.[9]

---

9 I received some of Mom's medical records. They were extensive. Progress notes, communications, messages, patient history, clinical findings, diagnostic test results, lab requisitions and results, pre and post-operative care, chronic ailments, physicians' orders, billing, and health insurance information.

Mom's diagnosis chart read: depressive episodes, osteoporosis, arthritis, chronic kidney disease, renal failure, hyperlipidemia, Alzheimer's disease, fracture of neck of femur, nonorganic psychosis, and possible aphasia.

Meds on her chart included: Memantine, Quetiapine, Sennosides A & B, Venlafaxine, Vitamin D, Fleet Enema, Calcium, Aricept, Bisacodyl, Risperidone, Acetaminophen, Tamiflu, Seroquel, Lorazepam, Loperamide, Ramipril, Quinidine, Ativan, Prednisone, Ventolin, Keflax, Montelukast, phenytoin, salbutamol, oseltamivir, and Prolia PFS—all of which (except a few) I had no earlier indication of what they were or what they treated.

Mom's records also stated that she could be physically aggressive and verbally aggressive which is common with an Alzheimer's diagnosis. I felt guilty and sad when I read, "Resident misses her family. Resident has some sad facial expressions and flat effect." A big punch to the gut. The more I read the less I knew her.

Cause of death; a) pneumonia, septicemia b) dementia-advanced, and c) COPD

After reading through hundreds of pages of medical notes and records, I know Mom was in great hands with the nurses, support staff, and doctors who cared for her all those years.

I am grateful.

We pulled up some chairs and talked to Mom, hoping at some level she'd know us. Weirdly, within minutes Brian and I quickly switched from talking to Mom to talking about Mom. How much she'd changed since Alzheimer's arrived. How subtly the changes happened; from forgetfulness to occasional confusion, and socially inappropriate comments and behaviors.

Mom wasn't a fan of foul language in ordinary conversation— although she'd use it from time to time. But with Alzheimer's, Mom consistently swore like a sailor. Like the time my sister Brenda and her daughter Rachel visited Mom not long after she was admitted to her first care home facility Leisure World.

***

"Mom, what are you doing?" Brenda asked. She winked at Rachel—because they knew exactly what Mom was doing.

"Folding things. For the babies. This is bullshit. I want to go home. This is fucking bullshit. I don't know why I'm here. So much bullshit around here. The doctors lied. I was supposed to start work already. This is bullshit. I can't stand hearing all these babies cry. Such bullshit."

***

Once they returned to the car, eight-year-old Rachel said,

"Gramma was swearing a lot. Why was Gramma swearing so much? She said that word so many times I started to count and she said bullshit forty-seven times!"

"I know—but remember even though Gramma was saying that, it wasn't really Gramma."

Pretty sure Rachel was confused with the answer. I wouldn't have been surprised had she muttered under her breath "Well, that's bullshit."

***

While Brian and I were in Mom's room, and she dozed in her chair, we also spoke about the time I discovered Mom wearing her underpants over top of her pants— three pairs of pants, that is.

***

"Hey, Mom. How are you feeling today?"

"I'm not sure. Something doesn't feel quite right."

"Well, you look nice. Did you pick out your clothes?

"Oh, did I? I don't remember. I must have. These are my clothes though, right? They feel a bit odd."

"It doesn't matter Mom. It's okay. Maybe we can adjust you a bit. You've got your panties on the outside. They should be first, next to your hoo-ha!"

"My what?"

"Your hoo-ha," I point.

Mom raised her eyebrows and looked at me, "Oh, I think I lost that."

I would've burst out laughing had I not realized Mom was dead serious.

"I used to be good at this." She blows a little puff of air.

"No worries, Mom. Let's just straighten things out a bit. So how about we switch the order of these layers, and we'll find a matching pair of socks? Sound good?"

"Thanks for helping me, dear."

"It's okay, Mom. We all need a little help sometimes. You're doing great. Let's get you feeling comfortable and looking fabulous again. But I won't be helping find your hoo-ha!"

"My what?"

***

After a few laughs and more discussion about Mom's journey, Brian and I reluctantly realized she definitely was in the later stages of the disease.[10]

It was a vicious reality. We looked at each other sadly and turned our attention back to Mom.

I found her hairbrush and started brushing her hair. Brian played music on his phone. He played songs from artists such as Ella Fitzgerald, Louis

---

10 The 7 Stages of Alzheimer's Disease:

Stage 1: Before Symptoms Appear. Normal outward behaviour.

Stage 2: Basic Forgetfulness. Very mild changes.

Stage 3: Noticeable Memory Difficulties. Mild decline.

Stage 4: More Than Memory Loss. Moderate decline.

Stage 5: Decreased Independence. Moderately severe decline.

Stage 6: Severe Symptoms. Severe decline.

Stage 7: Lack of Physical Control. Very severe decline.

Armstrong, and Frank Sinatra. At first, Mom was quiet and still stared into space, but when the music started, her eyes wandered, and she faintly hummed. She responded. She seemed calm. Her whole body seems to relax. [11]

"Hey Brian, play Rhinestone Cowboy."

Brian raised his eyebrows and shook his head, "Uhm, not sure that's a good idea."

"Just try it!"

Okay, I'm a bad daughter. I know this song has an unpleasant history with Mom, but I'm curious to see her response, if any, to this particular song. Could it possibly have some effect on her?

Even with Alzheimer's clouding her mind, Mom reacted to the song. As Glenn Campbell poured his heart out, Mom became more rigid, she grit her teeth

---

11 Touch can help Alzheimer's patients by calming them. One research that included 68 nursing home residents with dementia showed that the people who got hand massages for 10 minutes showed significantly reduced anxiety than the patients who got no medication. Touch can help communication without depending on words. Touch in caregiving can consist of hand lotion massage, hair combing or brushing, manicures, shoulder hugs, high fives, handshakes, or even a pat on the arm. (www.rightathome.net)

ever so slightly, her eyebrows angrily knit together, and she tried to raise her head.[12]

Both Brian and I had wide eyes, and our mouths hung open. Seriously! This little song was now an accidental experiment and a testament to the enduring power of certain memories—her hatred of *Rhinestone Cowboy* must be etched into the very core of her being. Brian quickly switched the song to Frank Sinatra crooning *Strangers in the Night*.

Mom relaxed, her body sank back into her chair, her eyebrows unknit themselves and her body became calm again. Frank's voice transported Mom back to a softer, gentler place in her mind.

It was both reassuring and heartbreaking. This song had such a powerful emotional impact on her, but her children's presence? Nothing.

I hoped somewhere deep inside she still knew how much we love her.

It's so hard to watch her forget how she loves us.

---

12 Music memories often remain in the brain even as language and other memories disappear in dementia. This is because regions of the brain that are involved in musical memory and processing (e.g. the cerebellum) are not as affected by A.D. or dementia until much later in the disease course. Thus, patients can retain the ability to dance and sing long after their ability to talk has diminished. (Northwestern Now- Research and Innovation)

And I hope she doesn't curse us for playing that damn song.

***

I've added a few more stories to Mom's eulogy. So close to the finish line now. Good thing—her service is tomorrow. Later today we go to the funeral home to decorate the chapel for her service.

I gather my papers together. I realize I don't have a copy of her obituary from the *Hamilton Spectator*. After all, it's what led to her instant international viral fame!

"Hey, Brenda," I yell toward her kitchen. "Do you have a copy of Mom's obituary from The Spec?"

"Yah, I bought several. Here." She hands me one.

I flip to the obit section. I find Mom's crazy photo and her lengthy obituary. I glance at the other obituaries on the page.

I gasp and blurt, "Holy shit!"

"What?"

I show Brenda the obituary page.

"What?" she asks, a little more exasperated.

"Check out the guy beside her. He died on the same day as Mom!"

"Okay, so?"

"Read his name!"

Brenda looks again at the page and starts howling with laughter.

"No waaaaaaaay!"

I laugh and shake my head. I glance back at the paper clipping and read his name again.

"Glen Campbell."

Now, this gentleman wasn't thee Glenn Campbell but he was still a Glen Campbell.

There's some serious karmic shit going on here, Mom.

Glen Campbell beside Mom in the newspaper.

October 6, 2004

Dear Barb,

Your father took me to the doctor today. He said I have something like almonds, no, that's not it. He said Alzheimer disease. Yes, that sounds important. Yes that's what he said. But I most certainly do not.

He made me do some tests. Your dad just looked out the window or at the docter. Then he went out the door.

I felt as though I was a little child in school. I have a digital clock not a round one with numbers.

I think he was trying to trick me because he asked me to count backward. I got flusterd and wanted to cry.

Sometimes I forget things but don't we all as we get older? How will I know I am not me anymore?

I saw you this summer, didn't I? Do you think I am losing my mind? I am too young. That is something old people get.

How are your childran?

I will be going to see my mother soon. I haven't been to the farm house in a long time.

I can't find my nursing ring? I know you wanted it. Did you take it? I think Barbara took it. She always wanted it.

Love,

Mom

CHAPTER 14:

OUR ROCK IS CRUMBLING

"Almonds" I sigh shaking my head. Her decline is so evident in this letter.

I put Mom's letter back in my bag. Reading it left me with a heavy heart. I remember reading it for the first time all those years ago—my reaction now feels the same as the first time—like a sucker punch to the heart.

It was like a dark cloud looming over our lives, threatening to steal away the memories Mom held dear—not knowing which ones would be taken first must have been incredibly distressing for her.

Mom was the rock of our family, the one who was always there to offer guidance, love, support, and of course, laughter! We felt so helpless knowing she was about to face such a formidable opponent as Alzheimer's.

Her letter served as a stark reminder of the fragility of life and the inevitability of change. I know she was determined to fight holding on to those memories and her identity.

I always knew she meant business when her nostrils flared. I sensed her nostrils flaring through her letter. More so when she was certain I had taken her nursing ring.

Over the years she would tell everyone and anyone that I had taken her ring.

I had taken it. But I took it with permission from Dad and that was only a few years ago.

Mom's nursing ring.

***

"Here, I found this in one of your mother's old socks."

Dad handed me her nursing ring. "Oh! You found it, Mom always thought I took it."

"We both knew that when she was gone you wanted it as a keepsake. She is not gone but in a sense she is gone. I know her accusations weren't true. It was the disease talking. I just didn't know where it was—until today. You should take it before it's lost forever."

I put the ring on and tear up. It fits perfectly.

Now I understand. Mom had hidden it herself, in a desperate attempt to safeguard it, only to forget where she'd put it.

I felt a flicker of reassurance maybe subconsciously she remembered I wanted it, even amidst her confusion.

"Dad, so maybe somewhere deep inside she must have remembered I wanted it if she thought I had taken it—so there's that."

"Yes, there's that."

***

Mom was haunted by the suspicion that her loved ones were stealing her cherished possessions, so she resorted to covertly stashing them away for safekeeping. Money and old letters were tucked in the pages of her books, jewelry hidden amongst her socks and underwear, random pieces of paper, and old receipts made their way into the pockets of her old winter coats, unaware that her mind was the ultimate thief, not her family. Alzheimer's was thieving her memories with each forgotten hiding place.

Aw, Sybil.

CHAPTER 15:

OUR DEAD CELEBRITY WITH THOUSANDS OF FANS

I grab a fresh cup of coffee and sit back down to write. My pen poises above the empty page—and thankfully, thoughts and words finally jump in my head: *larger than life, funny, spontaneous, creative, kind, and smart*…the words keep popping.

Everything just pours out of me.

I find myself grappling with the immense challenge of encapsulating the complex tapestry of her life within a few brief words. How to capture the laughter she shared, the meaning behind her flaring nostrils, the wisdom she imparted, her love of hummingbirds, her propensity for giving soapbox lectures and her countless acts of love, into a eulogy.

I want to weave a tribute to the numerous lives she touched and the effect she's had on all those she met. It's like squashing a rainbow into a tuna can.

***

My pen finally meets the paper:

When a person dies what do you say about them? How do you choose which pieces of their life are important enough to be shared in their eulogy and be wrapped up in five to seven minutes? I guess there's always the standard: she was born, she was a nurse, she married, she had a family, she had Alzheimer's, and she died—OR— will it be a bit more fun?!

I smile at this —since everyone at the funeral knew Mom, or read her obituary, I plan on making it much more fun!

***

Brenda walks into the living room wearing a huge smile,

"You won't believe this. Mom's obituary in the Hamilton Spectator was tweeted by Jim Poling—it's going VIRAL!"

I look up... "Huh?"

"Just Google "Sybil Hicks Obituary!"

I hit my laptop, and I'm laughing and crying a few minutes later.

A gazillion images of Mom pop up. Line after line of media links fill the screen. There are so many posts, tweets, shares, and articles! So many comments! It's surreal.

I get sucked in— and go down a rabbit hole for hours.

Here are just a few of the worldwide media that did a story on Mom:

The Irish Post

"OBITUARIES ARE supposed to be sombre affairs full of heartfelt tributes and expressions of sadness at the loss just experienced. But Sybil Hicks from Hamilton in Canada decided to do things a little differently when it came to the formal announcement of her own passing."

Metro, UK

"Obituaries aren't usually fun reads. But one Canadian grandmother decided to prove that even in death, she's hilarious."

CBC Radio —As It Happens

"Why 'smoking hot' Sybil Hicks' kids honoured her with a cheeky first-person obituary."

New York Post

"Woman pens her own hilarious obituary. "Sybil Hicks wrote the most hilarious first-person obituary in which she insulted her husband, her children, and had the last laugh-or so it seemed."

**REDDIT•Posted by
u/EtOHMartini:**

"This woman's obituary (Hamilton Spectator) proves that in death, she is funnier than I am in life..."

Fox News

"Sybil Hicks of Baysville, Ontario, went out with a bang after she wrote her own obituary saying she finally had the "smoking hot body I have always wanted...having been cremated."

My Tributes Australia

"Hicks's obituary appeared in the Hamilton Spectator on Feb. 5 and she has now become a posthumous social media celebrity. Sybil Hicks wrote the most hilarious first-person obituary in which she insulted her husband, her children, and had the last laugh — or so it seemed."

UpWorthy

"Her children, realizing that a traditional obituary wouldn't capture their mother's lively spirit overshadowed by Alzheimer's disease, decided to write a humorous first-person obituary."

Twitter

"We didn't deserve you," another tweet read.

"Best obituary award goes to Sybil Marie Hicks," read another.

PINTEREST

"Woman's obituary gets the last laugh with a cremation joke: 'I finally have the smoking hot body I have always wanted…having been cremated. The Ontario native's parting words are going viral."

Our mother is now an instant worldwide dead celebrity!

CHAPTER 16:
THE OBIT THAT ORBITED THE WORLD

Published by The Hamilton Spectator from February 2 to February 9, 2019.

HICKS, Sybil Marie (nee Lyons)

It hurts me to admit it … but I, Mrs. Ron Hicks from Baysville, have passed away. I passed peacefully with my eldest daughter, Brenda, by my side February 2, 2019 at 8:20 a.m.

I leave behind my loving husband, Ron Hicks, whom I often affectionately referred to as a "Horse's Ass."

I also left behind my children whom I tolerated over the years; Bob (with Carol) my oldest son and also my favourite. Brian (with Ginette) who was the Oreo cookie favourite, Brenda AKA "Hazel" who would run to clean the bathrooms when she heard company was coming. Barbara (with Gordon) the ever Miss Perfect and finally Baby Bruce (with Yasu) who wouldn't eat homemade turkey soup because he didn't want to be alert looking for bones while he ate.

I will miss seeing my sweetest grandchildren; Caitlin, Megan, Joel, Issac, Mason, Rachel, Annie, Emma, Harrison, Clark, Choe, Orion, Griffin … grow up to be the incredible people they are meant to be.

I graduated from Waterdown High School with honors while wearing my shiny bright saddle shoes. I later graduated from Hamilton General Hospital School Nursing class of 1957B — Best Class EVER!

In 1972 Ron and I loaded the car with the 5- B's and headed north to run a school bus company for over 20 years in Baysville, Ontario. I was an active horticulturalist, a member of the Eastern Star, and a member of the Lion's Club in Baysville.

I finally have the smoking hot body I have always wanted … having been cremated. Please come say goodbye and celebrate my wonderful life with my husband and his special friend Dorothy who is now lovingly taking care of my horse's ass.

For those of you who are wondering who assisted me in writing this … it wasn't my husband, it wasn't my oldest, nor was it my youngest … Thank you all for sharing my life with me.

I am off to swim to the buoy and back.

Love,

Sybil

hi sweety

where are you idontknowwhereyou are now
you are always sumwear else

I forget things life feels ~~dif dipher~~
strange

dad is hear to

i am a nurse

lov mom

p.s.

And the letters stop.

CHAPTER 17:

A LAST LETTER AND THE LAST SUPPER

That was the last letter I ever received from Mom. Dad was kind enough to mail it to me. He mentioned he found it on the rolltop desk and when he asked Mom about it, she insisted he was supposed to have mailed it.

***

"Why didn't you mail it?"

"I didn't know I was supposed to. I don't even remember you mentioning it."

"I'm sure I told you." Her brow furrowed as Mom tried to recall. "I'm sure I told you, Ron. It was important."

Irritated, Dad says, "Sybil, you're always forgetting things. Maybe you didn't tell me."

Mom became teary-eyed, "I did tell you. Why don't you believe me?"

Dad sighed, "It's hard for me too when you forget things. I will mail it right away."

***

Dad didn't mail it right away. He told me about the encounter between them. He didn't want to leave Mom at the house by herself.

Mom forgot about it again.

The erosion of Mom was palpable. Damn you, Alzheimer's.

Not sure I would've gone to the trouble to mail the letter. But I'm glad Dad mailed it—even though it's officially the saddest piece of mail I've ever received in my life.

Mom was still thinking about me on some level, and it demonstrated her significant decline. It was another punch to the gut.

I couldn't hear her voice with this one. It read as though someone else had written it. The spelling errors and the simplicity of it didn't exude any hint of Mom. Except for the nurse part.

I carefully refold it and put it in my bag. I still wonder to this day what she wanted to say in the P.S.

Time for supper with my family. You've heard of the rehearsal supper before a wedding? It weirdly feels like that. Although we're all preparing ourselves for a funeral.

The restaurant's atmosphere is a paradoxical blend of sorrow and laughter. With so many of us around the table, (and many of us haven't seen each other in years), our light-hearted moments create an unexpected contrast to the heavy emotions surrounding tomorrow.

Passersby who glance at our table see the animated gestures, shared laughter, and the clinking of glasses — are completely unaware of the poignant reason behind our dinner. A typical Hicks family gathering: lots of people with dry humour, and playful sarcasm—our shield of resilience. It protects us from sad or uncomfortable situations.

Grief lingers at the table but can't interrupt the infectious energy.

The menu is an unexpected source of comedy. Several dishes bear funny names. We start creating names for some of the dishes. It's a simple game that reflects Mom's playful spirit and love of quick puns.

"Mom's Marvelous Meatballs" and "Heavenly Hug Chicken Soup." These clever culinary creations are a tribute to Mom's personality. Suddenly, every order is an opportunity for us to share anecdotes about Mom's cooking skills and disastrous kitchen moments. Her many turkey mishaps; her finger getting caught in the mixer; the coffee mug exploding in her face, and when she dropped a four-gallon jar of Italian dressing on the brick floor; fallen cakes, boiled hamburger, and stinky burnt cheese in a cast iron pan…the list is endless.

As the evening unfolds, Mom's presence seems to linger around our table.

Our faces and stomachs ache from the laughter.

As for the grief? We've done our best to starve the fucker to death.

***

Mom enjoyed eating out—perhaps because it gave her a break from the kitchen prep for a big family and the dreaded clean-up. It always felt like a special treat because we didn't do it often. One time, just Mom and I had gone for lunch after a doctor's appointment. It was extra special for me because I was missing school. I must have been around fourteen. I had my learner's permit but I couldn't drive myself yet. Mom was my co-pilot.

"Well, this is a nice little spot, I've never been here before."

"I think it's new," Mom said. "But the chairs feel a bit wiggly. Or maybe it's just me?"

"Kind of, they remind me of the chairs you see in movies, you know—the ones with 'director' on the back."

Our lunch arrived. Mom had a vegetable stir-fry and I had a clubhouse sandwich. We chatted about school, summer plans for work, and my return to school in the fall.

Mom dropped her napkin. She needed to put on her glasses to see where the napkin had disappeared. Her glasses were hanging by a silver chain around her neck. Once she'd put them on, Mom looked at me and I burst out laughing.

"Mom, you have broccoli in your glasses."

"So, I do."

She sat for a minute staring at me, giving me plenty of time to take in this hilarious moment. The broccoli floret remained wedged between her eye and the lens of her glasses. Mom finally pulled it out, ate the rogue broccoli, and cleaned her glasses—laughing all the while.

Remembering her napkin had fallen, she leaned slightly to her right to pick it up. It was close to the chair leg. I watched her lean over, then lean over a bit more until she tipped over completely in her chair. Her arm was wedged between the floor and the arm of the chair.

I puzzled for a moment. Mom was there and then she wasn't. I stood up and peered over.

"Mom? What are you doing? Get up! This is embarrassing!"

Mom laughed and snorted at the same time.

"I can't! My arm is stuck—I've fallen, and I can't get up." And she started laughing again.

People were gawking. Being a typical teenager, I was embarrassed until I realized—*Mom was stuck!*

The waiter rushed over to help Mom, as did a few men from nearby tables. With all the grunting and groaning and maneuvering, she passed wind which set her off into fits of laughter and more snorting. I put my head down trying to hide both my embarrassment and amusement.

"Oh, my gawd, Mom!"

By this time, all eyes in the restaurant looked in our direction.

Mom was now standing, and the waiter asked about her arm.

"I'm a nurse. It's fine. Just my daughter's ego was hurt. Thanks for your help, gentlemen."

"Oh, my gawd, MOM!" I said rolling my eyes. "Can we go?"

Mom pointed to her plate and said, "Sure, when I'm all done all my broccoli."

***

I'm back at the hotel after supper, finalizing the eulogy and going over tomorrow's arrangements.

Brenda has asked the Lady Shriners to prepare the luncheon. The chapel is decorated, and David Bond, the funeral director has all he needs. Reverend Barnes is aware of the time, and all guests have directions to the funeral home.

I crawl into bed. Tomorrow will come fast.

This was the first time I've prepared for a funeral—I have no idea if anything is missing.

Well, except for Mom. She's the only one missing. Literally and physically.

The people who are coming to the funeral tomorrow?

They don't need to know one small detail.

Mom won't be in the box.

I guess she gets the last laugh!

CHAPTER 18:
MOM'S M.I.A. AND AN EMPTY URN

Walking down memory lane is a long walk uphill. I keep running into Mom and Dad. So many memories. So many conversations. So many antics. I enjoy writing, but eulogy writing isn't exactly a picnic.

GAH! I can't finish this right now. We're headed to the chapel to "decorate" for Mom's service tomorrow. Just how does one decorate for such an event? Where's Martha Stewart when you need her? Should we go for the bohemian funeral look? The modern funeral home look? Or the shabby chic funeral home look?

"Retro Restful?" "Serene Sarcophagus Chic?" or "Eternal Elegance?" Mom would have turned naming the funeral style into a game! With her dark humour—she'd have won.

Mom was a collector of eccentric treasures, crafts, and antiques—from Raggedy Ann dolls with mischievous grins to antique dishes and teacups, old furniture, and dried flower arrangements. Their home was a museum of quirky delights.

"Mom always did have flair for the dramatic," Brenda says as she holds up a particularly flamboyant (ugly) feathered hat she'd made as part of a costume for Dad. We roll our eyes and smile.

The chapel is a sombre place—we get that, but Brenda and I are determined to inject Mom's lively spirit into the room. Armed with a carload of Mom's crafts and heirlooms, our mission is to turn the chapel into a memorable place fit for a celebration of Mom's extraordinary life.

***

"Hey, where's Mom's urn?" One of my brothers asks.

"Oh, about that," I say. "The crematorium has a bit of a backlog. Who knew that could be a thing? So, Mom won't be returned to us for a few weeks."

"What? Are you kidding me?"

"Nope—looks like we'll be using her empty box. No one will ever know."

We laugh, realizing with Mom's love of the absurd, she'd probably find her delay amusing. Besides, she was late her entire life. And the fact we're holding her funeral and she won't be here? She'd find it side-splittingly hilarious!

Mom's urn is plain but pretty. It's a small two-toned pine box inlaid with flowers and a hummingbird— Mom loved hummingbirds. It's perfect and we all love it.

Undeterred that Mom won't be joining us, we haul in a variety of antiques, lots of flowers in old crockery—some dried, some fresh; the small faded pink wicker rocking chair she used as a small child; paintings she created, a few of her favourite books, and other plush toys Mom had sewn over the years.

We display photos of Mom's life along with the printed comments from people worldwide who've posted in response to her viral obituary. No one will believe how many hundreds of thousands of people have read her obit!

After a few hours, we survey our efforts. The chapel is transformed into a whimsical display of Mom's talent, fun, and quirkiness. She may not be here in urn form, but her spirit permeates the chapel in every oddity and eccentricity we've lovingly arranged.

Right down to the ink pad for all who attend, with instructions to press their right bird finger into the pad and press it next to their names in the guest book.

If they haven't already heard the ink pad story— they will—tomorrow.

Mom is nowhere to be found.

Brenda picked up mom's ashes and took her for her favourite
Tim Hortons coffee and fruit explosion muffin. She's baaack!

CHAPTER 19:
MY FOUR SIBLINGS AND A FUNERAL

I stir in the hotel bed. I wake up slowly to the realization that today isn't just an ordinary day.

Today is Mom's funeral.

Can it still be called a funeral if there's no body? I think about it briefly. If there's no body or cremated remains, maybe it's called a memorial service.

What did we call it? Service, I think?

Oh, well, it doesn't matter. It's too late now.

I groan, rub my eyes, and mutter to myself, "Well, this is one way to start the day."

As I stumble into the small bathroom, I can't help but think of the eulogy I've written for Mom. I hope it does her justice and reflects her love, her ability to live out loud, and her unique sense of humour.

Mom always said, "Life is too short to be serious all the time". She was so confident and could always laugh at herself. I admired that in her. No shame, no embarrassment, she just smiled through it all. Something I did NOT inherit. Hence my nickname, "Miss Perfect" perhaps?

***

We arrive at the funeral home a little earlier to ensure everything is ready. The sombre atmosphere feels uncomfortable. We need to start some peppy music! I made a playlist with a few fun "Mom" songs, a few folk ones, and a surprise song for when we exit. Meghan Trainor's Mom song suits Mom's spirit and Sarah McLachlan's, *I Will Remember You,* is fitting both for a service, and because Mom didn't remember us in her last years.

The songs play in the background as guests drop in for Mom's viewing. Some stay for the service and some leave. Perhaps they've discovered Mom isn't here?

I glance around at all the gorgeous flower arrangements and read the comments from the senders.

The messages are thoughtful and loving. And then suddenly—one of the messages bowls me over.

"OMG!" Where's Brenda?"

I spot her and quickly cross the chapel. I grab her arm. "Come with me. Did you see this one?"

She looks at the card and then at me. "Unbelievable!"

On the card is a lovely note of sympathy from the Reddit Community—in the United Kingdom. Obviously, they've seen Mom's obituary online. Like hundreds of thousands of people around the world this past week.

Wow. Wow. Wow.

Aw, Sybil—I'm not surprised. You're still making friends even when you're dead.

***

Friends and family gather in the pews, their faces are etched with sorrow. I'm happy I decided to channel Mom's spirit and infuse some humour into this weird day. The crowd has no idea what's coming!

After Reverend Barnes gives a few words, I walk to the podium and clear my throat.

"We're here to celebrate the life of Sybil Hicks. A woman who taught me everything—especially how to find humour in the strangest places."

I share funny stories and quirks about Mom that bring smiles and bursts of laughter from the mourners.

I can see by the looks of family and friends with their puzzled glances, that they're wondering if they've accidentally walked into a stand-up comedy routine instead of Mom's funeral.

At one point, the funeral director steps in to listen, and he grins. He's probably seen his fair share of solemn ceremonies and came in to see what all the laughter was about.

Mom's eulogy ends like how I wrote her obituary— in the first-person narrative— with Mom speaking to each of my siblings and Dad.

I can't help but imagine Mom smiling as she looks down on her unconventional farewell. And knowing Mom? She's probably standing right beside me with a whipped cream pie in her hand.

She always knew how to lighten the mood!

Later, as my sister laughs and cries, she scolds me, "You spoke long enough! That was like an hour!"

Well, how the hell do you squeeze a woman like Mom into fifteen minutes??

***

CHAPTER 20:
A QUIRKY EULOGY FOR SYBIL MARIE HICKS

I'm Barb Drummond, Sybil and Ron's fourth child. The adopted child—otherwise known as Mom's favourite child. Right, Bob?

When a person dies, what do you say about them? How do you choose which pieces of their life are important enough to share in their eulogy and be wrapped up in five to seven minutes? I guess there's always the standard: she was born, she was a nurse, she had a family, she had Alzheimer's, and then she died—OR — will it be a bit more fun?

Since everyone here today knew Sybil —or if you read her obituary, you know it has to be a bit more fun!

Mom didn't die on February 2, 2019. She died approximately eighteen years ago when the first signs of early onset dementia appeared and was formally diagnosed shortly there after.

All of us who are gathered to pay our respects to Sybil Marie Hicks have been touched in some way by Sybil's love and charm.

I am truly sorry for your loss.

Sybil was known to her children as Mom, or the favored endearment—Sybs. A term given to her by Brian who couldn't get her attention in the grocery store one day after calling "Mom" a thousand times. Yet when he called, "Sybs!" she immediately turned with raised eyebrows, "Yes?" As a result, the name stuck among us five children over the years.

Mom was also known by another name, one she adorned herself with, when she spoke on the phone to try and elevate her status, or to let them know she was damn serious! "This is Mrs. Ron Hicks from Baysville calling!" Upon hearing those words, we'd either know enough to leave the room or be nosy enough to stay. Needless to say—we usually stayed.

No matter what your term of endearment: Mom, Sybil, Sybs, Mrs. Ron Hicks or Sam (a name Dad called her, but we never discovered why?) Want to fess up now, Dad? No? She won't know you spilled the beans!

Mom relished the fact she had so many names from the people around her…she knew she was important to us—more importantly, she knew she was loved.

Sybil Marie Lyons was born in Burlington, Ontario on May 11, 1937, with dark hair, chubby cheeks, and undoubtedly, a wide smile! It was evident she was a wonderful combination of Harold and Elsie Lyons.

Mom was raised with good grounding, a lot of love, a lot of teasing, and a lot of tormenting by her brothers with a whole bunch of shenanigans to boot!

Can't you just hear her giggling with Gramma Elsie right now? Or hear her squeal "Ooohhhh" as Grampa Harold's deep voice welcomes her into his arms?

I'm sure she has already called Uncle Bruce, an "old bugger" after he greeted her with some smart-ass comment.

Upon hearing of Mom's passing, the five of us kids started reminiscing and reminding each other about

Sybil stories. During the time we were growing up, we didn't realize we were making all these memories. We thought we were just having fun.

Brenda tried to pry information from Dad about their life before having children—Dad wasn't forthcoming so it must be information not intended for a family audience.

We remember hearing something about Dad working at Uncle Albert's garage where he pumped up Mom's bicycle tire—apparently, that was all it took. Dad must have done a really good job with that tire, because he won her hand and the worm farmer guy —did not.

Mom and Dad's wedding anniversary will forever be engrained in our minds. How could it not? Whenever anyone asked when they were married, Dad would reply…SAY IT WITH ME NOW…

"Since October 4th, 1958, seems like yesterday— and you know what a bad day yesterday was."

Mom and Dad adored each other. Often when they kissed, the five of us kids would pretend to throw up and make barfing sounds.

The boys would say, "Oh, come on, rent a room!" and once Brenda said, "Yah stop, or the next thing you know you will be boinking!"

Mom laughed and she said, "You don't want us to WHAT?"

You know, "BOINK," Brenda replied with air quotes.

Mom laughed, then snorted, and replied, "Oh you kids say the craziest things."

We thought that was the end of that…but if you knew Sybil at all, that was not the end. She tucked this bit of information in her brain and somehow the term would pop up again when we least expected it.

Sure enough, a few weeks later Mom and Dad were both heading up the stairs. Brenda asked, "And where are you two going?" Mom replied with a serious face, "Upstairs to BOINK of course!" Brenda's face scrunched up and she replied with a loud "EEEEWWWW, gross!"

Well, it didn't stop there. Moments later we could hear something from their bedroom.

Okay, hang on…it's not what you are thinking. Good grief …this is a funeral!

Well, Ron and Sybil were upstairs yelling "BOINK BOINK BOINK!" at the top of their lungs…so we ran upstairs to their bedroom. Mom had taped a sign to their closed door that read, "The Boinking Room!"

Mom was like that. She would remember details of a situation, a comment you made, or an item you mentioned once in passing that would inevitably end up under the Christmas tree for you, or wrapped and ready for your birthday.

I remember shopping with Mom in Orillia the last summer I was back from university and said, "Oh, when I get married this is the tableware set, I would get!" Sure enough, when Gord and I married, that EXACT set appeared as a wedding gift.

I truly don't know how she did it.

But that WAS Mom, wasn't it? She was always over the top…for everyone and anyone.

I remember her giving big parties for all the grandchildren. One, in particular, stands out—not sure of the occasion, but Mom had invited Darryl and Lynne Hollingsworth out to sing and perform in our front yard. I remember big puppets, live music, food, and a LOT of laughter!

I remember one Christmas when Mom showcased her incredible baking talents by creating a breathtaking array of gingerbread houses. The house smelled divine with cinnamon wafting into all corners of the house. Mom baked and decorated twenty gingerbread houses, each one a unique creation. It took her hours and hours to bring them to life with intricate designs and sugary adornments. And the crowning jewel that year was the gingerbread farm she crafted for the Armstrong family. But much like the baked goods she prepared for the church bazaar, we weren't able to indulge in her creations.

Mom's gingerbread houses.

When Mom and Dad moved the family to Baysville in 1972, we didn't realize at the time what a fantastic place in which we were raised. Initially, we moved into the "white house. "That's what we called it as kids…when friends asked where we lived, we'd say, "We live in the white house, not THAT White House, just a white house"—we would laugh and laugh.

A few years later (I'm sure Brenda will know the date), we moved into what Mom called her DREAM house. It was a big five-bedroom house on the Lake of Bays, at the end of Strathheid Road. I remember Mom and Dad renovating that house. Some of the renovation was due to a change in décor, however, it was mostly due to an infestation of large carpenter ants! Walls upon walls were full of them. On a positive note, the source of the strange noise in the walls was discovered.

I'm sure you won't ever witness a crazier renovation crew than with the Hicks-Kosmack carpenter crew. Come to think of it, they were more of a beer crew with a carpenter problem.

Mom and Dad loved to go to auction sales and were avid antique hunters. You just never knew what was going to appear after they returned.

After one such trip, they returned with a table with seven leaves that created a very long table—twenty-one feet if my memory serves! That table came in handy on many occasions. One night we had our dear friends, the Armstrong family, over for dinner along with a few others. As always, lots of food, drinks, and laughter. Each leaf was inserted in the table, and it stretched across the room. The people on the far side of the table were trapped—there was no way out on either end of the table—once they were in…they were in! So, in true Hicks fashion, many people ended up UNDER the table to get out!

That night, fortunately for our guests, turkey wasn't involved. Perhaps, you've already heard of Mom's infamous turkey stories. This story once again involves the Kosmacks and the Heggies and Brenda's (Hazel) new Gloria Vanderbilt blue jeans as I recall. Her jeans were almost done being washed, and the water began draining into the laundry tub. Brenda didn't realize Mom had placed the turkey to thaw in the wash tub. Aunt Mary witnessed the results and came running out of the laundry room screeching, "The turkey is blue, the turkey is blue!"

Just so you know, when a blue turkey is cooked, it doesn't taste that different.

Now, picture this one Christmas. Mom was making Christmas dinner for the whole family when the oven stopped working. Our neighbors John and Barb Able offered up their oven since they had their feast the night before. Mom loaded the turkey on the toboggan and took it to the neighbors. On the return trip with the turkey all cooked and ready to eat back in the toboggan, Bruce showed up with his girlfriend. Lisa asked, "Sybil, what are you doing?" Mom replied, "Oh, Lisa, don't you know? It's Hicks tradition to take the turkey for a sleigh ride before you eat it."

Mom taking the turkey for a ride in the snow!

As you all know, Mom was a brilliant lady and there wasn't much she couldn't do. One of Mom's many talents was her ability to sew—her creations were amazing. The laundry room was sewing central for her sewing and other craft items. My friend Mary Sue remembers Mom teaching her how to sew. Mom was so patient. I remember her teaching me to sew and I got so angry and tossed the fabric on the laundry room floor with a few potty words. Mom asked me what the problem was. I remember answering, "Because I can't do this, I can't do this like you can—I want to be just like you!"

Bruce lightened the mood by asking, "Just how many sewing machines does one woman need?"

Speaking of sewing machines…Mom had asked Dad to pick up some needles for her machine…he went into the store and asked for needles for a Boeing 747. Dad called Mom to confirm. Mom roared and said, "I have a Bernia 740, you horse's ass!"

***

One of the most favourite of Mom's interests was gardening. We all remember Mom gardening or growing flowers for the Horticultural Flower Shows. She had the greenest thumb ever! She would even garden in her swimsuit so when she was finished gardening, she could go down to the water for her MOST favourite thing in the whole wild world…a swim in the lake. Her swim was always to the buoy and back…often more than once.

Recently, I wondered if Mom could talk before she passed—what would she have to say to each of us.

Bob, I am so proud of you. Raising your family in a life led by God with a beautiful wife who shares your values. You have raised wonderful children together. You are a fellow with many talents, a love for cars, and an eye for antiques! You have my mother's ability to talk to anyone. You have a laugh like no other.

Yes, Bob, you are my favourite.

Brian, I am so proud of you. You have had tremendous changes in your life and have been successful and adventurous with Ginette by your side. You have wonderful children who possess your strength and their mother's beauty (Wendy). I appreciate Ginette's joy in life and her ability to support you in reconnecting with those who are important to you. Even if your life has taken you further away, I have always felt your presence —no regrets— I appreciate the times you were able to visit.

Yes, Brian, you are my favourite.

Brenda, yes, I am so proud of you. You are one hell of a cook and cleaner—sorry had to say that, Hazel! You have such creative talents that are reflected in your cozy home. You are a gifted hairdresser and have such a great sense of sarcasm and humour! You wear your heart on your sleeve and give to others so freely. You are stronger than you will ever know and have done well raising a beautiful "Mini – Brenda" single-handed.

Yes, Brenda, you are my favourite.

It took me a bit to think of what Mom would say to me, I knew she was proud of all of us. I think she would simply say, "Barb, look in the mirror and know you are your mother's daughter."

Yes, Barb, you are my favourite.

Bruce, I am so proud of you. My Baby Bruce, I know you didn't like my homemade turkey soup because you didn't want to be alert in case you might encounter a bone.[13] Just so you know, I didn't like it either. You're the only one who can make me laugh from head to toe. You have had a life like no other and I'm so proud of the man and father you have become. You're funny, intelligent, and kind, and will always be my baby.

Yes, Bruce, you are my favourite.

---

13 Bruce was always worried about choking on a turkey bone in the homemade turkey soup. He told Mom he didn't like homemade soup because he didn't want to have to be alert to eat it!

My dear Ron,

We've had quite the life together. We have five wonderful children, lots of friends, and many adventures over the years. Even before October 4th, 1958! I have no regrets. Our life together was lived fully.

I am happy that you've found companionship with Dorothy.[14] I know how much you need people around you. I always told the kids, "If something were to happen to me, never deny your Dad companionship"—well, I guess something happened.

I love you and you will always remain— my horse's ass.

---

14 Who's Dorothy? Well, when Mom's obituary went viral around the world—so many people asked, "Who's Dorothy?" Followed by some wild comments and ferocious speculation. Please remember, Mom had Alzheimer's for eighteen years. For many of those years, she was navigating the challenges of progressive memory loss with intermittent bouts of forgetfulness with fleeting moments of clarity. Then the relentless progression led her into the realm of profound memory loss where her once vivid and intimate connection with Dad and us kids faded away until we disappeared from her mind completely. Mom's journey took her into the hospital, into a care facility, and then another care home until her death in 2019. Dorothy loved Mom too. They'd known each other for years. Dorothy had been married to Mom's cousin. Dorothy understood Dad's love for Mom. She did what she could to support Dad through such a lonely, emotional, and challenging journey.

So there! Hopefully, that stops all the gossip! Good grief!

CHAPTER 21:

COUSIN BARRY AND THE EGG SALAD SANDWICHES

There are advantages to funerals. You get to see people you haven't seen in years and everyone is pretty dressed up. And then, once the funeral is over? You get lunch.

After solemn funeral ceremonies, mourners often find solace in the comforting ritual of post-service luncheons, where a spread of delicate, crustless sandwiches are a symbol of communal support.

Really. It's one of the best reasons to go to a funeral.

All the delicious food is crafted with care by the nurturing hands of the church ladies. In our case, however, they were made by the lovely hands of the Lady Shriners.

And the baking? No store-bought crap allowed. Homemade squares like the ones your mom and grandma made, wait on plates with doilies. Brownies, Hello Dollies, lemon squares, peanut butter and marshmallow squares, and more, load down the tables. Are you drooling yet?

And one thing is for sure. There's going to be a pile of hungry sad people waiting to hoover it all down. Confession. I'm usually at the front of the food line. Well, except this time.

My cousin Barry beat me to the front. Why?

Well, he knows what the star of the funeral show always is—the egg salad sandwich.

And any solid funeralgoer knows, homemade egg salad funeral sandwiches are always the first to fly off the table.

Today is no different.

The egg salad sandwiches are the first to be devoured, much to my favourite cousin Barry's obvious disappointment. The revered egg salad sandwiches have eluded him. Somehow, the other funeralgoers have jumped the gun on him. He has to settle for ham.

"Don't get me wrong, I loved Aunt Sybil, but I love egg salad sandwiches more. Sometimes, I go to funerals just for the egg salad sandwiches." Barry's kind eyes twinkle all the while.

I burst out laughing at his priceless comment— Mom was fond of Barry and would've appreciated the timing of his words.

She would've laughed— then snorted.

My entire life, every time we saw Barry, he'd greet us by saying, "Hi, how is my favourite cousin?" and then turn and say the exact words to my sister and brothers. It was a running joke in the family, and he never failed to make us laugh.

And I do feel bad that he's missed out on the egg salad sandwiches.

Mom and our "favourite" cousin Barry.

***

The atmosphere in the basement is more sombre than in the chapel upstairs. I look around the room and see old and familiar faces. Many people are smiling and chatting, and others sit in uncomfortable silence.

As I make my way around the room wanting to visit as many of those faces as possible, I can't help but wonder, *Is it weird to think funerals are an emotional collision? Painfully sad but happy at the same time.*

I encounter childhood friends I haven't seen in decades. The nostalgia of shared memories floods our conversations, bridging the years that kept us apart. It was as if the sadness of the moment has prompted a collective journey back in time, where the laughter comes out as if we're kids again!

As I continue making my rounds, I realize the small village of Baysville, which we'd called home, was well-represented with friendly familiar faces from my youth. There was an unspoken comfort— reminding me that a community, no matter how many years apart, can still provide solace and support.

***

"I remember the time we had the whole village out looking for you! Your Mom was frantic."

"I remember that." I tear up and smile at the memory. "I'd fallen asleep under Mom's antique singer sewing machine on the wide foot pedal. It was my favourite spot to read."

"Your mom was so relieved, but she wasn't sure if she should spank you or hug you once you were found."

Just for the record, she hugged me.

***

I encounter unfamiliar faces—people who'd been friends with my parents, extend their condolences with heartfelt stories of the years they'd spent together before I was born. It was touching to hear how my mom had impacted lives beyond our immediate circle.

As the crowd slowly dwindled, I can't help but feel a twinge of disappointment. No one has shared any scandalous or juicy stories about Mom. I chuckle to myself, realizing it's probably for the best. I've shared enough of her shenanigans. Any secrets, or skeletons if there were any, will remain with Mom.

With a wistful smile, I make my way towards the exit, I know it's too late to hold anything over on her now anyway.

One thing I make a note of for when I finally leave the planet— there needs to be two million homemade egg salad sandwiches.

I'll make sure to add it to my will.

And Barry, since I'm much younger, you'll probably miss out on those too.

CHAPTER 22:
EDDY THE CAT
AND THE UNTIMELY FART

After Mom's service, the Hicks kids pile into various cars to meet back at Brenda's. It's a bit of an ordeal. The old pecking order is reinstated, and the arguments over who gets the front seat echo our youth.

The ride starts quietly until out of nowhere, a suspicious sound is heard —a muffled but unmistakable noise from the back seat.

"Who did that?" Brenda asks as she peers into her rearview mirror.

"My bet would have been on Dad but he's in Brian's car!" I say.

The car's back seat turns into a blame game battleground. Fingers quickly point at each other. A collective gasp fills the car as the odour finally reaches the front.

"Ewwww, smells like egg salad sandwiches!" I say while covering my nose, prompting everyone to roll down the windows in a synchronized panic!

Rachel points a finger at me.

I roll my eyes, "Please, like I would ever…wait, was that you, Bruce? Yes, it was you!" I point toward him.

Bruce says, "Uhm, dunno—maybe?" He grins widely and innocently looks out his open window.

"Remember when Mom used to do dishes after supper? Every time she bent over to load the dishwasher, we heard her toot from the living room!"

"She'd laugh, snort, and fart some more!"

And there you have it, a typical conversation from the Hicks family. A bunch of well-educated, mature adults. Do we discuss politics or world events?

Nope—farting.

***

We gather in Brenda's quaint and cozy living room decorated with flair like Mom and Dad's home. The drinks flow, and the last remnants of the chapel luncheon are spread across the table—but still no sign of the elusive egg salad sandwich.

As we reminisce, more forgotten stories from our youth are remembered and shared. Each story triggers another.

"Remember the time Eddy the cat ate Brenda's hair ribbon?"

"Oh, Eddy! Right, Mom named him Eddy because he was always falling asleep—just like Mr. Armstrong."

Mr. Armstrong was a long-time family friend. He and Dad would get into all kinds of mischief. We giggled over him falling asleep. Mr. Armstrong was always falling asleep. He worked hard and slept hard.

The Armstrongs would be over for supper and dessert hadn't even appeared when snores started from the far end of the table—Eddy was asleep again.

Once he fell asleep while on the phone with Dad and, even the air horn didn't wake Mr. Armstrong up!

"Oh, don't remind me. Poor cat!" Brenda scrunches her nose, "But I really wanted to wear that ribbon to school, and it was hanging out Eddy's bum!"

I can barely tell the story I'm now laughing so hard!

"Mom put on her yellow rubber gloves. She picked up Eddy in one hand, grabbed the ribbon with the other hand, and tossed the cat in one direction, and pulled the string in the other!"

Panting for breath I finish, "The cat's eyeballs grew twice their size…he let out a yowl…a sound I'd never heard before … off he ran… faster than a bullet!"

"Mom had a pained look on her face as she was worried she'd "re-arranged his intestines.""

"We didn't see Eddy for weeks after that!"

By this time, we're all in stitches, holding our sides and covering our mouths!

Brenda offers quietly, "Just so you know, I didn't wear that ribbon to school."

Fits of laughter start again, tears streaming down our faces.

***

More and more stories pop up; night skiing with a candle for a headlamp; when Mom gave Whiskers, our old bubble-gum-chewing sheepdog, a haircut with her sacred sewing scissors; too many rums and coke with the neighbours next door; the chimney fire; as well as the 'never-to-take rides from strangers' spiel.

"I'm going outside now, Mom."

"Okay, remember, don't take rides from strangers!"

"Mom, I'm going to the woodpile."

It's ironic how adamant Mom was about us never taking rides from strangers. Because in the throes of Alzheimer's she'd wander off and end up in a car with someone who knew her but she didn't know them— essentially strangers.

***

Immersed in our laughter-filled trip down memory lane, we hear a knock at the door. We open it to find Cousin Barry and his daughter Ginny on the stoop —wearing big smiles.

"Brenda invited us over. Any chance for an egg salad sandwich, I missed them at lunch today?" Another mischievous twinkle from Barry as his eyes glance over the spread on the table.

"Sorry, Barry—you're out of luck."

Barry and Ginny stay for a brief visit before heading back to Hamilton. It's so nice to connect with family—despite such circumstances.

As the evening winds down, we decide to capture the moment with a family photo, not knowing when we'll be together like this again.

We start to assemble ourselves as Bruce places his phone on photo burst mode, so we'll have a range of photos to choose from. He hands the phone to Dad's friend Dorothy to take the photo.

Of course, just as the camera begins to click continuously to freeze our moments in time—we hear the sudden unmistakable sound of Dad letting out a triumphant, albeit untimely—fart.

Our collective "ewwwwwws" echo through the house as we cover our faces! Our picture-perfect moment is hilariously tainted by Dad's unexpected contribution.

But we can't help but appreciate the irony— the night ended how it started.

Family photo.

...and then Dad farted.

CHAPTER 23:
IF ELLEN CALLS, I'M TALKING TO HER!

My day starts slowly and lazily at the hotel. I sip a few strong cups coffee and enjoy a delicious breakfast of eggs and bacon. Why does breakfast taste so much better when someone else makes it?

I walk into Brenda's just after nine. The air outside is crisp, so stepping into her home feels extra cozy.

Brenda hands me another coffee and I say, "Hey, morning. Are you tired from yesterday? What's going on today?"

Ignoring my question, she responds with, "You're not going to fucking believe it."

"What??"

"Have you checked your email or social media? I've been getting messages non-stop!"

"No, I just enjoyed a leisurely morning and didn't have my phone on."

"That's rare—you without your phone. Go get it, you've got to check it out. NOW!"

**

When I penned Mom's obituary with a few ideas from Brian and Brenda, I wanted to make sure I gave Mom her voice back one last time. It was to be her final goodbye. And it worked. Her voice and character came across loud and clear!

We were adamant that Mom deserved more than a cheesy obituary boilerplate: she was born, she lived, and she died.

Brenda said, "Mom wasn't an ordinary person so she can't have an ordinary obituary!"

Little did I know how writing it in the first-person narrative would strike a chord with thousands of readers around the world.

The media frenzy started with Jim Polling, editor-in-chief of The Waterloo Region Record when he tweeted "The last word, Obit in today's @Spec" and he shared Mom's obituary that was published a few days before in The Hamilton Spectator on February 6, 2019.

Following his initial tweet, Mom's obituary went viral on social media, touching the hearts of thousands of people from different ages, cultures and backgrounds worldwide. It was strange and wonderful.

Even after death, she was bringing people together.

For a day that started so slow, it was about to become a harried frenzy!

Brenda is getting texts and messages from international and national news outlets requesting interviews, and my email is blowing up for more information. Newspapers, television stations, and radio shows all want to hear Mom's story and the inspiration behind the quirky obituary.

I'm dumbfounded by this unexpected media attention. In the days leading up to her funeral, we've witnessed some social media interest from the obit, but nothing to this extent. Even after the funeral— this thing has taken on a life of its own! (Okay, I know that sounds funny when you're talking about an obit.)

Brian is the family-spoken person since no one else jumped at the chance.

However, I make it very clear, *"If* Ellen DeGeneres calls, *I'm* talking to her!" Just the thought of talking to Ellen puts a smile on my face.

Brian's relishing the spotlight, acting like a seasoned television star. The only thing missing is the little bib stars wear to stop make-up from getting on their collars, otherwise, he fits the part. He's charismatic and well-spoken. He speaks like Mom did— when she was on her soapbox, with wise authority and a bossy tone—the role suits him.

"Okay, Brenda, you reply to the messages and set up some more phone calls. Barb, reply to the emails. I have an interview with Carol Off from CBC Radio later today. She's the host of *As It Happens!"*

I think he said it out loud just to hear it for himself— we already know who Carol Off is.

Brian jokes, "Have your people, call my people."

Off he went to Brenda's room to talk to—well, more people.

***

The day is becoming a whirlwind!

What a once in a lifetime opportunity to share Mom's story. The three of us orchestrate interviews and manage schedules—the chaos is hard to direct.

Bob, Bruce, and Dad sit in the living room and watch the insanity unfold.

Dad is on the overstuffed armchair surfing his iPad and reading the occasional comment out loud.

"I'm guessing that Dorothy is the family dog. I think she's having one last joke at the expense of her husband." Dad reads. "It was from someone called the at sign *dazcolumbo*."

Bruce laughs and tells Dad all about the @ sign and what it mean when printed on social media. I'm impressed Dad is even on social media at eighty-seven years old.

Dad starts reading again, "I was standing in the post office reading it, laughing out loud, wondered what people who came in thought about the person laughing at an obituary, she sounds like she really lived her life." And then Dad adds, "But she didn't have an at sign, just her name Judy B."

The male trio laughs.

"Another lady wants to know why the Melissa McCarthy photo—any special connection?"

The lady was referring to the crazy photo of Mom in her old retro glasses, her hair was a disaster, her head was tilted, and she had a crazy look. Many people think it's a photo of Melissa McCarthy —the famous Hollywood actress.

I say, "Just tell her Mom had her face long before Melissa McCarthy did."

***

In the afternoon, we have an interview booked with a news station in the US. The name escapes me, there are so many being thrown at us. But this station wants to interview us live to be broadcast later today. This adds an unexpected layer of chaos to our already hectic schedule.

Bruce sets up his phone on a bench stacked with books, while the four of us sit lined up on the couch in birth order. We save his spot at the end so he can jump in once the camera is recording.

The interview is a complete disaster.

The interview takes a surreal turn as technical problems plague the call. The line drops repeatedly; the disjointed conversation becomes a strange dance of connecting and reconnecting and trying to pick up where we left off.

It feels bizarre—like an unrehearsed performance with a glitchy soundtrack. And true to form, as in situations like this, we start to giggle—which always seems to happen in the most inopportune times. We've never been through a media shitstorm before, and this interview is a gong show.

Needless to say—the interview never aired.

Thank God.

***

Brian stands up and checks his watch, "We've got to reply to these texts and emails promptly." His authoritative voice sounds like Mom's when she tried to organize us for school in the mornings. "We can't let anything slip through the cracks!"

As the interviews continue and the social media comments reach a fevered pitch, we try to navigate the fine balance of grieving privately and the desire to share our incredible mom with the world.

We know once the media madness subsides, the ringing phones go silent, and the emails from eager reporters dwindle—then we can sit and process the events of the day.

From his chair, Dad voices his gratitude for the outpouring of love and support he's received from us and strangers around the world. Dad is usually a grumpy old fart so we're all blinking back tears.

We spend another hour or so reading and sharing comments. In the pauses between the words, we take moments to share laughter, tears, and a few more anecdotes about Mom.

This unbelievable strange legacy for Mom is unexpected and she'll endure long after her media spotlight fades.

***

We say our goodbyes that night, all five B's are heading to our homes in the morning. Bruce will spend a few days with Dad and Dorothy, Brian heads back to Toronto with Mason for a longer visit, Bob and his wife are heading back to their home, and I have an evening flight back to Alberta.

"Mom would have loved this." Brenda says.

"Yeah, Mom got an incredible send-off, didn't she?"

"My house is going to be so quiet now."

With a mixture of gratitude and weariness, we disperse.

This whirlwind experience has been weird, fascinating, and exciting—and so odd because we're grieving at the same time.

But one thing I know for sure. We honoured Mom in a way that truly celebrates her remarkableness. And she'd have absolutely loved the craziness of it.

But damn you, Ellen. You didn't call!

CHAPTER 24:

REFLECTIONS AT 37,000 FEET

My flight is called to board.

I'm early to my gate. I'm always way too early. I laugh thinking it must be my superpower. I don't like being late or feeling rushed—so— early it is.

With the long wait over, I get up to board with the rest of my zone people. I glance around to see if my seat partner from a week ago is also boarding. I hadn't asked for his name, but I remember his mom's name was Catherine. Catherine with a C.

I speculate how his mother's funeral went.

Mmm? I wonder if her body was part of the Ontario crematorium backup as well.

No sign of Catherine with a C's son.

As the airplane ascends into the evening sky, I'm lost in a whirlwind of emotions.

Just a week ago I came back to officially say goodbye to Mom and help give her a send-off into the next existence—whatever that might be.

It's only been a week but it seems much longer. I miss Gord and our kids. I have a four-hour flight and then a five-hour drive before I can lay eyes on my family and give them hugs.

Mom battled Alzheimer's for what felt like an eternity to me—eighteen years. I wonder how time felt for her. It must have felt like an endless prison. She was trapped in the hell of Alzheimer's. There are so many jerks in the world who deserve to get Alzheimer's, but Mom certainly wasn't one of them. She was one of the good guys.

Actually, Alzheimer's is so horrid—I wouldn't wish it on *anyone*.

During those eighteen years, she wasn't my "real" mom—that mom started dying with her diagnosis. The woman who ended up in the nursing home became someone else's mom. I feel like I've been without my mother for almost twenty years. And I've needed her so much.

This has been a tumultuous and yet strangely cathartic journey. Hearing and sharing stories of our "real" Mom was healing—and it's left my real Mom in my mind instead of the more recent images of the other mother. The one who didn't know me or love me anymore.

Mom's friend Cindy describes her as a "quiet bomb". They were partners in crime for saving this or that, or setting examples as good citizens for many different causes.

I chuckled at her description—Mom wasn't always quiet.

***

"Yes, hello? I need some toilet paper!"

Pause. The yelling starts again.

"Hello? Anyone? Help! I need some toilet paper!"

Another pause.

"Help! I need some toilet paper! I'm in the short bathroom! There's no toilet paper! Hello!"

Sometimes Mom was in such a rush to the bathroom she didn't check for toilet paper until after sitting down. We've all been there!

We heard this toilet paper soliloquy more than once during our childhoods.

Boy, could she yell.

Quiet bomb, indeed.

***

Watching Mom fade away piece by piece has been a heart-breaking ordeal—one filled with grief, guilt, and a constant sense of helplessness.

But amidst the pain, there's also been moments of unexpected joy—a laugh, a spontaneous smile, or an intense goodbye hug. These fleeting glimpses reminded me she was still Sybs.

I think about the time this past week I've spent immersed in the bittersweet task of writing her obituary and eulogy. I combed through letters and photographs; shared stories, asked questions, listened to others share memories, and reminisced about happier times—her healthier times.

But thinking about Mom and her journey is terrifying.

Do I carry the gene?[15]

---

15 APOE 4: the APOE gene, if present when tested, increases an individual's risk for developing late-onset Alzheimer's disease in certain populations. Having the gene doubles or triples the risk of getting Alzheimer's.

1. National Library of Medicine. APOE gene. https:// medlineplus. gov/genetics/apoe/

Do I want to know?

I grapple with the decision.

I have for a long time—ever since Mom's diagnosis.

How would I have handled the news had it been me?

Alzheimer's is like a fading tapestry, the threads of memory slowly unravel, leaving behind a patchwork of confusion and loss.

Over the years we witnessed Mom's unraveling. A woman who had once been the cornerstone of our lives underwent a painful transformation that defied comprehension. It's a surreal nightmare watching someone lose their mind.

Unfortunately, the destruction of Alzheimer's is real.

A woman who used to prep an emergency room now prepped sandwiches she'd made with old, dried tea bags. Her once gentle demeanor became flashes of anger and aggression. Like the time she accused our son of hitting her with a two-by-four—but he wasn't even there.

Her moments of lucidity were overshadowed by episodes of paranoia and confusion. Accusations of stealing and infidelity. She was tortured.

Our once familiar faces became strangers in her eyes, and our names were lost in the labyrinth of plaques and tangles of her mind.

On particularly bad days, her erratic and unpredictable behaviour was calmed with Seroquel.[16] Mom would float off into deep relaxation and everyone sighed with relief for her and us.

I recall the day I realized her blank stare meant she truly didn't know us. It felt like a knife in my heart. Mom's eyes could still see but they weren't seeing. I wonder if her mind was protecting Mom from the pain of not knowing who we were.

I turn and stare out the airplane window into the darkness. I can't see anything out in the night as we fly over the clouds. Is this how Mom saw the world during those two decades?

Surely with Mom's positive attitude, she'd have looked to find patches of silver linings.

I wish I could have asked her—but it's way too late for that.

Now that Mom's battle with Alzheimer's is over, I must be content with the memories we shared, the laughter she created, the lessons she taught, and the love she gave.

And I'm also grateful she's died.

---

16 Seroquel: antipsychotic medication sometimes used in reducing agitation in elderly Alzheimer's disease patients.

My gorgeous and vibrant mother is finally released from the fucking Gulag prison in her mind.

I hope she threw a pie in their face or flipped Alzheimer's the bird on the way out.

Now Mom's physical presence is gone and her ashes will reside in a hummingbird wooden box on display in my sister's living room. Mom will hold court in the antique china cabinet that previously belonged to her and Dad. The very same glass-fronted cabinet we were to never go near as children.

Mom's spirit will live on in my heart for as long as I'm able to remember. She gave me life and she changed my life.

I lay my head back on the airplane seat and close my eyes.

I wonder what Mom's up to now.

—I'm pretty sure I just heard a snort behind me.

Aw, Sybil.

I love you.

Thank you, Mom.

See you at the buoy.

EPILOGUE:

MY LAST SOAP BOX

Hi, it's me, Mrs. Ron Hicks of Baysville.

If you're reading this, I've embarked on the greatest adventure of them all, beyond the bounds of mortal existence.

Now that the fog has lifted from my mind, I want to share some insight from my journey with Alzheimer's.

It wasn't all bad.

If someone dropped by, someone whom I didn't want to visit with—I could fake memory loss, stare off into the distance, or get up and make dry tea bag sandwiches. That was sure to shorten the visit.

Or I could take off one sock and hand it to them or I could purposely put my underwear over my pants—big turn-off.

They always left in a hurry after that.

Seriously though. Life bestowed upon me the roles of caregiver, friend, wife, mother, and grandmother. It gave me the privilege of stitching wounds and hearts alike, of raising children who are now grown, and of witnessing the world bloom through the eyes of my grandchildren.

Yet, fate, or Murphy's law (whatever your belief) in its curious twists, led me down a path lined with memories that crumbled like sand through my fingers.

Alzheimer's, they call it—is a thief in the night, and it robbed me slowly of the treasures and people I hold dear.

But, oh how I fought! I wasn't going to let that old bugger take me down without a fight!

With every fiber of my being, I clung to laughter, to joy, to family and friends—to the essence of who I was.

I knew I was ill long before my diagnosis; I wasn't brave enough to admit it. I was good at hiding it.

After eighteen years fogged in by *the forgetting,* I discovered something always remains unbroken—and never forgotten.

It's love.

Love, my dear friends, goes beyond time and memory. It dances in the spaces between recollections, in the warmth or a smile, the touch of a hand, the gentle feeding at dinner time, in the warm conversations, in the reminders to take medication, or in the listening to music—except *Rhinestone Cowboy.*

That song still makes my blood boil. Barb, there was a reason the song didn't play during the end of my memorial. I stopped it!

You thought you were so sneaky.

To anyone reading this, facing your own battle with Alzheimer's or standing alongside a loved one who is, I say this: hold onto hope. Hold onto laughter. Hold onto each other. It is in our connections that we find strength.

As for me, well, I didn't remember all the details of my life, but I'll always carry with me the love and laughter that shaped me into who I was.

And in the end, isn't that what truly matters?

Embrace the laughter, even if you're laughing at tea bag sandwiches, or layers and layers of underwear.

Cherish the moments— perhaps when your loved one remembers your name, or when they complete a simple task.

Deepen relationships with whom you have lost touch.

Be grateful for the many caregivers, nurses, and doctors who are doing their best. But be mindful of the crushed pills in the pudding—they didn't think I knew. Sneaky buggers. That's an old trick I used on my kids.

Learn the true meaning of resilience and dare to look for it—it might surprise you.

Finally, find a new perspective and focus on what truly matters.

Love. Love matters.

So, as I bid you farewell, dear reader, I do so with a heart full of gratitude and a brain full of …well, who knows what! But fear not, because I've taken the joy of a good laugh with me.

While Alzheimer's may have stolen a few of my marbles, it never took my spirit nor my sense of humour!

Let's raise a glass of Carlo Rossi to the absurdity of it all, to the moments of forgetfulness that led to unexpected adventure, and to the love that remained steadfast, even when my brain decided to play hide and seek.

Laughter is truly the best medicine—even if you can't remember where you put the pill bottle!

To each of you who read and shared my obituary online and sent my humour and my spirit dancing—thank you!

It's quite fun becoming an international celebrity—even if I am dead.

Because remember, I now have the smoking hot body I have always wanted.

See you at the buoy!

All my love,

Sybil

P.S. So, just like your last chapter, Barb— this epilogue isn't that funny. But, if you remember, most of my soapbox lectures weren't either.

And finally, for the record—Bruce is my favourite.

ACKNOWLEDGEMENTS

Jim Poling. Thank you for your Twitter post that started it all!

Kim Duke, my editor and book coach, thank you for asking, "How badly do you want to write your book?" Your words of wisdom and encouragement are appreciated, but the red editing lines? Not so much. And, thank gawd I didn't give you any fork-in-the-eye moments none that I know of anyhow! Kim, you're fucking awesome. Want to do this again?

Brenda Hicks, you have been tremendous in supporting me on this journey. Thank you for answering all my texts, pestering questions, finding documents, and reminding me of dates and timelines. You have your father's mind for dates and information. Too bad I was adopted.

Gordon Drummond, my heartfelt gratitude for graciously putting up with my incessant writing, researching, movie watching, book buying, and podcast listening. Thanks for not abandoning me despite the countless times I canceled plans to stay in with my computer and a cold cup of coffee. We can go for those walks now.

To my kids, Annie, Emma, Harrison who encouraged me to write and listened to some of my excerpts – I appreciated it. Thanks for pretending to understand what I was talking about when I rambled on about neurons, synapses, plaques, and tangles and not rolling your eyes too hard. Clark, thanks for getting your own milk while I was typing madly.

Andy McEachern, thank you for bravely revisiting that harrowing snowmobile incident from 1979. Your willingness to share such an intense moment highlights the incredible courage of everyone involved that night. Your contribution honours Mom's memory in a truly profound way.

Dianna Havin. For your enthusiasm and excitement when I shared this book idea with you.

You inspired me. I know it is not like donating a kidney, but hey, this is big for me.

My reader, thanks for making it past the dedication page. You're clearly a person of great intelligence, great taste, and strange humour. I hope this book lived up to your expectations or at least provided a distraction from whatever you were supposed to be doing.

To those of you facing the Alzheimer's monster, or caring for loved ones—I wish you strength, love, and patience.

And to anyone who stumbled across this book accidentally and thought, *Well, I guess I'll give it a try*—thank you! May your spontaneity and curiosity lead you to even more literary surprises.

And to the people who told me I couldn't do it— you were wrong. But thanks for the motivation.

Love,

Barb

Published in the Bracebridge Examiner/shared on The Standard Marketplace

Hello, everyone! Sybil here. Or I guess you know me best NOW as "Mrs. Ron Hicks of Baysville"—the dead internet sensation!

I thought it was time to send my thanks…

To my caregivers at the Pines: you received me into your care not knowing the real Sybil, my former self, the Sybil before Alzheimer's.

You accepted me unconditionally: the confused me, the sometimes sad me, the quiet me, the rude me, the stubborn me, and perhaps sometimes …the angry me.

I heard the times you called me "Sybs" and "Dear". I heard you make chit-chat with me…respecting that I was more than just a body in the chair. I appreciated the times you directed me to dinner, rolled me to the activity room. The way you joked about finding the things I took from the other residents and returned them on my behalf. The time you took to label my clothes, the care you took in feeding me, how you bathed me, clothed me, and brushed my hair. You were respectful. It allowed me to keep my dignity…right to my end when I was completely dependent on each of you.

I had no way to express my gratitude toward you. No way to tell you that I noticed when you were having a tough day too… I wanted to return the comfort and tell you that everything would be okay.

Please know, I was proud to be one of your residents at Oak.

To Reynolds Funeral Home (Bracebridge): Thank you very much for guiding my family with such professionalism, proper funeral etiquette, and sincerity as they planned for my celebration. Being my offspring, I am sure it was not an easy task for you at times. I highly recommend your services to others…I know people are dying to get in…but hope they do not require your lovely chapel for many years to come.

To the Lady Shriners: Thank you so much for organizing and feeding my family and friends following my celebration. Red was one of my favorite colors and you all looked so caring and lovely in your red blazers. Just so you know …the egg salad sandwiches and the chocolate peanut butter stacks were a hit!

To the Alzheimer's Society of Muskoka: Thank you for educating those close to me about what to expect and how to care for me when I was making tea bag sandwiches, dressing in layers upon layers, and repeating my thoughts hundreds and hundreds of times a day. It was comforting knowing they had access to an amazing group with resources to lead them through my journey into Alzheimer's.

And finally, I would be remiss if I did not extend a thank you to **Jim Poling** @PolingRecord for spotting my obituary in the Hamilton Spectator and sending me on a world-wide cyber journey that was truly incredible.

I am in a place that is far beyond swimming to the buoy …a place that is beyond human understanding… truly powerful with profound comfort and intense love.

My heartfelt thanks to all.

Sybil

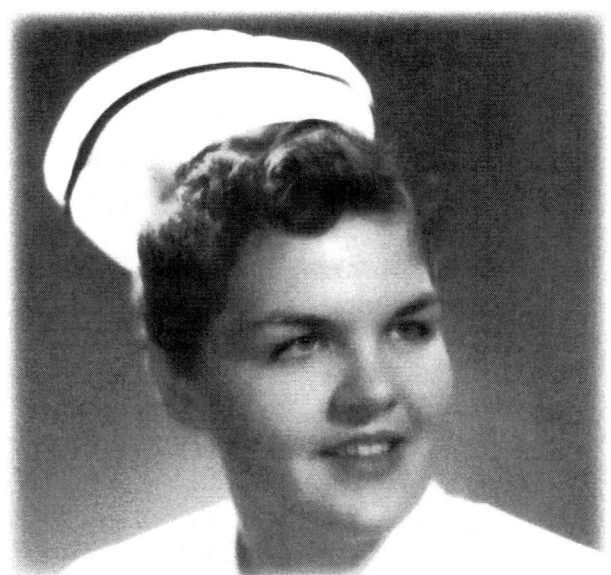

Mom's nursing photo-1957.

Because Alzheimer's Goes After Everyone
If Given A Chance

Sybil Hicks
Racquel Welch
Doris Anita Jones
Glenn Campbell
Auguste Deter
Charlton Heston
Margaret Thatcher
Graeme MacIntosh
Peter Falk
Perry Como
Bessie Hope Wolf
Jimmy Stewart
Rita Hayworth
Ray Dolby
Bob Barker
Iris Murdoch
Jack Lord
Adele Miller
Rosa Parks
Joyce Chen
Aaron Copland
Gabriel Garcia Marquez
Thomas Dorsey
B. Smith

Winston Churchill
Mary Doll
Lorne Mann
Gene Wilder
Ronald Reagan
Sargent Shriver
James Doohan
Tony Bennett
Joseph Garber
Burgess Meredith
Norman Rockwell
Joan Richards
E.B. White
Charles Bronson
Jack Hanna
Robert Bly
Gordie Howe
Louis Feraud
Sugar Ray Robinson
Harold Wilson
Estelle Getty
Barry Goldwater
Dutch Queen Juliana
Aaron Spelling

Pat Summit

Dana Andrews

Mike Frankovich

Arthur O'Connell

Edmond O'Brien

Otto Preminger

Harry Ritz

Arlene Francis

Mabel Anderson

Abe Burrows

Ross Macdonald

Robert Wilson

Ben Bradlee

Robert Huebner

John Douglas French

Fiona Phillips

Wendy Mitchell

Dr. Clair Hawes

And many, many, many more!

MEET THE AUTHOR

Barb Drummond

Barb Drummond wants to live in a world filled with inclusive education, access to essential services for our friends with diverse abilities; and where books come bundled with a mint chocolate bar and a killer cup of coffee.

Barb is a writer, author, speaker, guest panelist, and an award winner in both business and education.

When she isn't taking online courses, writing, researching Down syndrome or Alzheimer's —she's working with her husband to run their four Tim Hortons restaurants and an office complex. Barb is also a Board of Director for the Canadian Tim Hortons Foundation Camps.

She holds certificates in cutting-edge techniques and programs that strengthen brain function for people with cognitive weaknesses, trauma, and those suffering with memory issues. Barb is certified as an SOI Practitioner and an IPP (Integrated Program Protocol) Specialist as well as a TLP (The Listening Program) Provider.

Barb and her husband, Gord, won the Premier's Council Award for Employment Excellence with provincial recognition. They've demonstrated outstanding achievement and leadership in making positive changes that create inclusive, barrier-free communities where persons with disabilities can fully participate.

Barb and Gord live in Peace River, Alberta where their four children: Annie, Emma, Harrison, and Clark also live.

Barb's future plans are to write more books, and continue to advocate for people with Down syndrome, and those with diverse abilities. To advocate for humanizing care for the growing number of Canadians diagnosed with dementia. She wants to spread awareness by raising her voice and compelling policymakers at every level of government to produce real change for the Alzheimer's community. (She knows her mom is getting the cream pies ready!)

Oh, and she wants to get her master's degree, read more books, and maybe even learn how to take naps.

RESOURCES

Books:

- *The 36-Hour Day: A Family Guide to Caring for People Who Have Alzheimer Disease, Other Dementias, and Memory Loss by Nancy L. Mace and Peter V. Rabins.*

- *Still Alice by Lisa Genova*

- *The Memory Thief: And the Secrets Behind How We Remember – A Medical Mystery by Lauren Aguirre*

- *Somebody I Used to Know by Wendy Mitchell*

- *Slow Dancing with a Stranger by Meryl Comer*

- *Before I Forget Michael Shnayerson*

- *The 36 Hour Day by Peter V Rabins*

- *Dear Alzheimer's A Diary or Living with Dementia by Keith Oliver*

- *There's Still a Person In There: The Complete Guide to Treating & Coping With Alzheimer's by Michael Castleman, Delores Gallagher Thompson, PhD and Matthew Naythons, M.D.*

- *Dancing with Dementia: My Story of Living Positively with Dementia by Christine Bryden*

- *Where Memories Go: Why Dementia Changes Everything by Sally Magnusson*

- *Losing Everything: A Family's Journey with Alzheimer's by S P Murray*

- *Memory's Last Breath by Gerda Saunders*

- *Somebody Stole My Iron A Family Memoir of Dementia by Vicki Tapia*

- *Death in Slow Motion by Eleanor Cooney*

- *Remember by Lisa Genova*
- *Feeding My Mother by Jann Arden*
- *My Father's Brain by Sandeep Jauhar*
- *Tangles and Plaques: AMother and Daughter Face Alzheimer's by Susan Cushman*

- *A dignified Life by Virginia Bell M.S.W. & David Troxel M.P.H.*

- *Alzheimer's Daughter by Jean Lee*

- *The Man Who Mistook His Wife For A Hat by Oliver Sacks*
- *Neither Married Nor Single by David Kirkpatrick*
- *The Neuroscientist Who Lost Her Mind by Barbara Lipski*
- *The Mind of a Mnemonist by A.R. Luria*

Websites:

- Alzheimer's Association (alz.org): Provides information, resources, and support for individuals living with Alzheimer's and their caregivers.

- Alzheimer's Society (alzheimers.org.uk): Offers support, research updates, and resources for people affected by dementia in the UK.

- National Institute on Aging (nia.nih.gov/alzheimers): Provides research updates, clinical trial information, and resources for Alzheimer's patients and caregivers.

Research Journals:

- "Alzheimer's & Dementia: The Journal of the Alzheimer's Association": Publishes peer-reviewed research articles on Alzheimer's disease and related dementias.

- "Journal of Alzheimer's Disease": Focuses on research related to the causes, progression, and treatment of Alzheimer's disease.

Support Groups:

- Local Alzheimer's Association chapters often host support groups for caregivers and individuals living with Alzheimer's. You can find these groups through the Alzheimer's Association website.

- Online support groups and forums, such as those on the Alzheimer's Association's website or platforms like Reddit, can provide valuable peer support and information sharing. Search for ones that feel right for you.

Government Agencies:

- Centers for Disease Control and Prevention (CDC): Offers information on Alzheimer's disease, including risk factors, symptoms, and prevention strategies.

- National Institute on Aging (NIA): Conducts and supports research on aging, including Alzheimer's disease, and provides educational resources for the public.

Documentaries and Films:

- "Alive Inside" (2014): Explores the transformative power of music for individuals living with Alzheimer's and dementia.

- "Still Alice" (2014) Alice Howland is proud of the life she worked so hard to build. At fifty years old, she's a cognitive psychology professor at Harvard and a world-renowned expert in linguistics with a successful husband and three grown children. When she becomes increasingly disoriented and forgetful, a tragic diagnosis changes her life - and her relationship with her family and the world - forever.

- "A Head Full of Honey" (2018): A man suffering from Alzheimer's embarks on a final road trup with his granddaughter.

- "Iris" (2002) The true life story of novelist-philosopher Iris Murdoch. A young idealist with aspirations of writing meets and falls in love with her soulmate, John Bayley. But it's Bayley who stands in the shadows and supports his wife through everything, including her battle with Alzheimer's Disease

- "The Father." (2020) A man refuses all assistance from his daughter as he ages. As he tries to make sense of his changing circumstances, he begins to doubt his loved ones, his own mind and even the fabric of his reality.

- "What They Had." (2018) Bridget returns home at her brother's urging to deal with her ailing mother and her father's reluctance to let go of their life together.

- "Elizabeth is Missing." (2019) The film follows Maud's journey as she tries to understand a mystery about her missing friend, and how the mists of memory about a long-lost sister shape her experience.

- "Iris" (2014): A documentary about the life of Iris Apfel, a fashion icon who discusses her experiences with aging and Alzheimer's disease.

Clinical Trials Registries:

- ClinicalTrials.gov: Searchable database of clinical trials investigating potential treatments for Alzheimer's disease and related dementias.

Educational Programs:

- Alzheimer's Association locally, provincially, and internationally offers educational programs and workshops for caregivers and individuals living with Alzheimer's disease. These may cover topics such as caregiving strategies, communication techniques, and understanding the progression of the disease.

Medical Professionals:

- Consultation with healthcare providers, including neurologists, geriatricians, and psychiatrists, can provide personalized information and guidance regarding diagnosis, treatment options, and management of Alzheimer's disease.

Community Centers and Senior Centers:

- Many community and senior centers offer programs and services for individuals living with Alzheimer's and their caregivers, including social activities, support groups, and respite care services.

- The Hogeweyk—The world's first "dementia village", The Hogeweyk in The Netherlands, opened in 2009. It is world famous; inclusive; truly person-centred with high-quality care and treatment; revolutionary; groundbreaking;

disruptive; and sustainable, and it breaks the stigma of dementia. They do all this so that people with dementia can continue their lives in a world that is safe for them and open to everyone.

Podcasts:

- Let's Not Be Kidding—https://www.cbc.ca/listen/cbc-podcasts/1387-let-s-not-be-kidding-with-gavin-crawford

- Cognitive Connections: Conversations on Dementia—https://alzheimer.ca/ab/en/whats-happening/news/introducing-brand-new-cognitive-connections-podcast

- Dementia Together Podcast— https://www.alzheimers.org.uk/get-support/publications-and-factsheets/dementia-together/podcast

Donations:

- Alzheimer Society or Canada -Societe Alzheimer du Canada —https://www.canadahelps.org/en/charities/alzheimer-society-societe-alzheimer/

- Alzheimer's Association— https://www.alz.org/get-involved-now/donate

Manufactured by Amazon.ca
Acheson, AB

14763659R00139